NEW LAMPS FOR OLD

NEW LAMPS FOR OLD

A sequel to
THE ENCHANTED GLASS

By HARDIN CRAIG

BASIL BLACKWELL

OXFORD

1960

© Basil Blackwell & Mott Ltd. 1960

PRINTED IN GREAT BRITAIN BY
BILLING AND SONS LIMITED, GUILDFORD AND LONDON
H9644

To the Memory of Una M. Ellis-Fermor

PREFACE

MY BOOK, *The Enchanted Glass*, was published about a quarter of a century ago. In that book I attempted to discover something about the Elizabethan mind in literature, and by literature I meant almost everything that seemed to have a bearing on it—scholarship, criticism, creativity, cultural background with theories and beliefs, and even vagaries. I wished to discover the secret of renascence. I did not succeed, but I did perhaps point out some operative elements. I tried to tell these things to my contemporaries and succeeded perhaps in reaching some of them.

The Elizabethans, indeed the men of the Italian Renaissance, are old friends and associates of mine and it seems only fair that I should tell them about our mind as it occupies itself with these literary matters. We cannot address the men of the Renaissance directly, but they nevertheless deserve consideration, and, if we could reach them by written or spoken word, we should have to acknowledge that, for some still unknown reason, they, in spite of their disadvantages and shortcomings and of our vast superiority in everything that one would think matters, have the better of us. I cannot address the Elizabethans or, with any degree of safety, modern scholars and critics, who are often specialists and seem to have no need of the more general types of truth. I have therefore taken counsel of Diotima and decided to tell the simple truth as I see it to ordinary reading persons and to

vii

younger scholars. We are much more sure of ourselves than were men like Bacon, Hooker, Camden and Harvey.

Part of this pride comes from our unfortunate conquest by the scientific method in the later centuries. That method was never more than partly valid in our discursive field, and its positivism has been our bane. It is encouraging to note, however, that this positivism has been sternly rejected by the sciences themselves, and it may be that a younger generation in our field will escape. I have looked about to see if there is any outlet and have done a lot of very hard reading in the search. I have gone so far as to suggest that, with proper adaptation, the philosophy of relativity with its naturalistic theory of cognition might develop into a philosophy suited not only to humanistic knowledge but to humanistic creativity. What I have found is, I think, a subject worthy of consideration. I might state a series of general probabilities in this way: If it is true that the philosophy of an individual, a group or a people is, as it is said to be, the most important thing about them; if throughout the total environment truth is one, as Aristotle, St. Thomas Aquinas, Bacon and Einstein thought; if discursive fields (religion, philosophy, the social sciences and the humanities) do not lend themselves to experimental verification and must therefore perforce proceed inductively; and, finally, if the humanities would adopt a philosophy suited both to learning and participation,—there might be a distant hope for a cultural renascence in our civilization.

HARDIN CRAIG

Columbia, Missouri
21 March 1960

CONTENTS

NEW LAMPS FOR OLD

CHAPTER I

AN OPEN WORLD

> Nobody who has really gone deeply into the matter
> will deny that in practice the world of phenomena
> uniquely determines the theoretical system, in spite of
> the fact that there is no logical bridge between phe-
> nomena and their theoretical principles; this is what
> Leibnitz described so happily as a 'pre-established
> harmony'.—Einstein, *The Principles of Research.*

THE NEW epistemology rests on certain concepts and is by now fairly familiar to the learned
world. The first of these is the inseparability
of space and time in the process of thought in which
time is recognized as forming with the three dimen-
sions of space a union in the fourth dimension. This,
as our minds are constituted, is unintelligible, although mathematically easily comprehended. This
four-dimensional complex has been called a space-time
continuum. It is infinitely varied and designates environment in the widest sense of the term. As such, it
is inexhaustibly extensive.

Cognition, according to this theory, is an operation
in the fourth dimension, whose actuality has to be
accepted on other grounds than conscious observation.
The nearest we can come to it is to say that it has an
intelligible organization, stated, however, in rather
unintelligible terms: a three-dimensional space com-
bination meets, let us say in the mind, with a one-
dimensional time sequence, and an act of cognition

1

or thought takes place in the fourth dimension. This explanation does not in an ordinary sense explain. We can, however, argue that the operation is an entity, since it has an intelligible beginning and an intelligible related end. The middle, the major process, remains a mystery. This theory of cognition, to which no great attention has been paid, seems to have been taken for granted as a consequence of Minkowski's establishment of the space-time continuum, of which indeed it is a part. On this occasion the whole vast field of the theory of knowledge is left untouched, and the theory in question is merely used as a basis for certain inferences with reference to the investigation of discursive subjects.[1]

Cognition has always been a mystery, always the main cause of superstition and many other sorts of error and delusion. For our purposes in the study of literature we may say that, since cognition was a mystery, men have sought to account for works of the highest excellence in essence and skill seemingly beyond the range of human powers as due to divine intervention in the process of cognition. A variant of this invented cause is to put forward a claim for the existence of unaccountable powers called intuition or genius. The effect of the new theory of cognition is to close the gap and to say that, so far as one can see, there is no necessity for such fictions and no shop in which such superhuman agencies may do their work. An element from a physical situation comes in here that lends plausibility to the idea that man himself is capable of generating and performing the works attributed to his hand. There is, it seems, in the cells or synapses of the human cortex an ample provision for all that man has ever thought or executed. It is believed by scientists that the brain has in these minute parts provision for nine billion possibilities of ideation through the interrelations of brain cells. In any case, nobody has ever seen an angel come down from heaven and take the brush from the painter's hand or the pen from that of the poet. Probability seems to be on the side of the synapses.

This probability is not to be despised. It has the greatness of nature in it. It provides a great task, the comprehension and manipulation of the vast environment, and an instrument, generated by that environment through the ages, with which to operate. Indeed, it goes further than that. It takes care of itself. Indeed, to interfere with it too much is, as we shall see, to injure its operation by narrowing the range and to restrict it to formal and conventional channels. One thing that has not perhaps been noticed is that it is in line with the freedom of the individual. It has been becoming slowly manifest that the progress of the world, let us say educationally, is dependent on the numbers of individuals who can be induced to be themselves, to develop and exercise their own powers. The Greeks knew this and it sometimes appears in our age and time, although in general we believe in teaching and put stress on it instead of on learning.[2]

In discursive fields, which depend on the slow accumulation of wisdom through the patient observation of carefully tested particulars, great results might be achieved by a philosophy that puts the responsibility for human welfare squarely on human beings and by convincing them that God in his infinite wisdom has made simple and practical provision for human welfare and human progress, so that there is no value in contrivance or theoretical reorganizations of self-deception.

We in the humanities must recognize the variety as

well as the unity of all knowledge and free ourselves from superstition and dogmatism and, if possible, regain the individual freedom to which as children of God we are entitled. This is no recondite or abstruse matter. It is as simple as intelligent living. It means the observation and comprehension of particulars. This done, the whole matter is attended to so far as we are concerned. We need to know the nature of things, for the truth of fact is the nature of things. Our minds do the rest. It happens that in our case the relation of language and thought is primary, since language is at once the medium of thought and the composition of thought, the two being so integrated that they cannot be disjoined. This relation has been greatly exploited under the name of symbolization, semantics has also played a part, and the results are so important and so far-reaching that they cannot be safely neglected, since from the exploitation of symbolization we have come to an understanding of the process not only of intellection but of mental growth.[3] The process fits in well with what was said above of the almost unlimited possibilities of the brain in relation to the range and versatility of human achievement.

These ideas have made their appearance in the twentieth century mainly as a result of Einstein's discoveries and the work of mathematicians and philosophers who have contributed to the proofs of his theories of relativity and have amplified them into a philosophy. This has been cautiously done and is therefore still widely regarded as a philisophical system applicable only to the investigations of science. Some philosophers have, however, carried the newly created philosophy of relativity beyond the natural sciences into those less tangible fields described as discursive subjects. Their tendency is to make of it a philosophy of general application. Einstein himself believed in the unity of all knowledge, and, if relativistic principles apply to all knowledge, they apply to the humanities. This offers uncertain footing, but has been carried so far that it seems justifiable to consider it at least as a working basis, especially since the humanities have a great deal to show in favour of it. Our task is to make these matters clear, and we begin with a celebrated modern essay on Francis Bacon.

In 1926, on the occasion of the tercentenary of Bacon's death, Professor C. D. Broad made a clear and just assessment of Bacon's philosophy from the point of view of the scientific method, just as if Bacon had published *De Augmentis Scientiarum, Novum Organum, Sylva Sylvarum,* and the fragmentary outlines of the Instauratio Magna in the twentieth century instead of the seventeenth.[4] Broad decides that from the point of view of science Bacon is unimportant. Broad knew exactly what he was talking about, admired Bacon, and no doubt was fully aware of Bacon's larger aims, although Broad disregards them, and, if he thought there was any method by which they might be achieved he does not say so, and whether he thought there was any truth except that which is arrived at by controlled experiment we do not know. He merely shows that it was Descartes and his successors, and not Bacon, who were the founders and practitioners of science in this narrow sense. Broad's address occasioned some disappointment and even disagreement among those who heard it or read it, for the learned tradition had placed Bacon high in the list of scientists, indeed had put him on the level of Aristotle.

The matter is not difficult to understand, and it is a pity that Broad did not take the time and trouble, if he thought it was true, to point out that Bacon believed in the unity of all knowledge and hoped that on its completion the Great Instauration would arrive at absolute completeness. This issue, which is sometimes still not understood, seems most easily explained by calling attention to the simple fact that discursive subjects—theology, philosophy, large parts of the social sciences and the humanities—do not lend themselves fully, if at all, to controlled experiment and must therefore be approached in a different and less facile way, that is, largely by induction.

It has seemed to me and to others that Bacon, with his concept of the unity of all knowledge, was actuated by a broader concept than that derived from Descartes, which showed a disposition to regard truth derived from controlled experiment as the only certain truth. One wishes that Broad had written on Bacon's scientific and philosophical works in the light of the discoveries of Einstein and his followers, but he did not choose to do so. One feels sure that Broad would have seen obvious indications that Bacon was thinking on levels far in advance of his time and at least anticipatory of the latest non-positivistic system of the current philosophy of science. Neither Bacon nor any man of his age could have carried through such an enterprise as Bacon initiated. The whole area was merely confusion, and Bacon had the genius to begin at the beginning. One cannot even say that Bacon's theory was workable in any age, but the point is that it was an attempt to achieve an all-embracing concept.

This is not the place, even if I were able to do so, to criticize the attempt to rule Bacon out as one who during the following three centuries contributed to the advancement of learning, nor did Broad attempt to do so. He does, however, disregard, as if it were a negligible matter, the continued use of so-called Baconian induction for more than two centuries after Bacon's death.[5] This seems unfortunate in view of the fact that in general approach to knowledge induction is not widely out of line with the relativistic approach. But again one returns to the idea that discursive subjects do not yield completely, sometimes not at all, to experiment, and yet important truth is in those fields.

Broad says that Bacon was not aware of the function of the hypothesis, and this is true if one means the sharp-edged tool called the hypothesis by natural scientists. But of course the anticipation of ruling concepts is a natural and necessary process in all abstraction. In this sense Bacon made too many rather than too few hypotheses, more than he or any man of his time could have supported. It is also possible that Bacon's disregard of mathematics was in some sense due to the fact that his aim was the mastery of all knowledge, not merely that part which defended an experiment. The whole criticism of Bacon amounts more or less to the fact that he could not live in the sixteenth and seventeenth centuries and at the same time enjoy the knowledge and experience of the twentieth.

In considering the advancement of the philosophy of science Broad's criticism of Bacon ought not to be overlooked. He speaks discouragingly of progress in the general field of learning, but admits the possibility:

If the old methods are still to be used the prospect is dark indeed. Our intellectual powers are no greater than those of the ancients; our only advantage over them is in the additional experience which has accumulated in two thousand years. . . . Our only hope is to devise a new method which shall be to the mind as rulers and compasses are to the hand. The mere rationalists are like spiders who spin wonderful but flimsy webs out of their own bodies; the mere empiricists are like ants who collect raw materials without selection and store them up without modification. True and fruitful science must combine rationalism with empiricism, and be like the bee who gathers materials from every flower and then works them up by her own activities into honey.[6]

This statement is suggestive of profound truth, since it rests on actualities and relies on the mind. What I don't see is its variance from Bacon. To be sure, what Broad has left is a framework of ideas that constitutes a vast hypothesis to be proved.

Broad's treatment of Bacon's views on the relation between reason and revelation is a perfect statement of Bacon's views. These views provided a sort of by-pass or partial surrender by means of which Bacon might avoid theology and be free to operate in the world of fact. Broad's statement of Bacon's directions for forming a complete Natural History is perfect:

Nature may act either freely and normally or freely but abnormally, or under deliberate constraint of man.

In this Bacon's slight modification of a universally held Renaissance principle is of course most important for the history of science. These are the 'bonds of Proteus'. Another example of Broad's perspicacity is his statement that Bacon insisted 'that there is no essential difference between the natural and the artificial'.

Professor Broad next provides distinguished treatments of what Bacon called the Metaphysics of Forms, which he concludes is empirical science or theoretical physics; of the Science of Human Nature, which consists in the doctrine of Idols; and of the aspect of Ministrations to the Senses, Memory and Reason. 'Reason may be used either for discovering plausible arguments to persuade others or justify oneself, or in order to understand our Mother Nature.' As to the former purpose, Broad says, 'We may therefore leave barristers, preachers, and newspaper-editors in happy possession of so useful an instrument.'

At the end Professor Broad summarizes his criticism:

(1) Was Bacon a great scientist who discovered new facts and established physical theories which form the basis of modern science? Most certainly not.

(2) Granted that modern science does not owe any important facts or special theories to Bacon, does it derive its general methods and its general outlook on the world from him?

The answer is qualified:

If then Bacon be the father of the method and outlook of modern science he is so by spiritual affinity rather than by natural generation.

(3) Granted that Bacon's actual influence has been over-rated, did he in fact discover and state explicitly those methods and principles of scientific research and inductive proof which scientists implicitly use with so much success?

Considering the fact that Bacon's territory of investigation was far larger than that of natural science, the answer seems perfectly true and fair:

It seems to me that the honours of stating those methods and principles are pretty evenly divided between Bacon and Descartes.

(4) Lastly, did Bacon provide any logical justification for the principles and methods which he elicited and which scientists assume and use?

The answer is emphatic and seems to me to depend on what is meant by 'logical justification'. It depends on the interpretation of the history of philosophy and must be judged from that point of view by those who are competent to do so:

He did not, and never saw that it was necessary to do so. There is a skeleton in the cupboard of Inductive Logic, which Bacon never suspected and Hume first exposed to view.

The value of the essay is, however, in Professor Broad's clear statement of fact, and it makes no difference that his own belief seems to have been in the scientific method as the only known means of discovering the truths of nature. He deserves praise and not blame, for at the time at which he spoke clarity was the thing needed for further progress.

It has seemed to me that a normal educated man, let us say a scholar, having no specialized knowledge of philosophy, may by the use of natural faculties arrive at truth by the use of industry, caution, common sense and adequate knowledge. This would hardly be denied, and, if it is true, it seems that truth must be a correct understanding of nature in the wider as well as the narrower sense of that word. If so, a great scholar might travel, perhaps less dexterously, the same pathway to truth that a philosopher would travel. Although the two might not be intimately acquainted and would not speak exactly the same language, they might arrive at about the same place. At any rate, I should like to present by way of illustration the case of such a great scholar, the late Professor John Livingston Lowes.

The Road to Xanadu appeared in 1927, one year after Professor C. D. Broad's *The Philosophy of Francis Bacon*, to which we have just been devoting our attention. *The Road to Xanadu* is a work of broad, well-informed and interesting scholarship. It has no relation to Professor Broad's essay unless one grants that that essay is written strictly from the point of view of the philosophy of science—what is known as the scientific method—and even then there is little

ground for comparison; Lowes shows only casual consciousness or use of the scientific method as applied
to the study of literature, but proceeds inductively
in the examination of data and makes his generalizations on the basis of what he finds. The sheer erudition of the work is enormous, and the author brings
to it not only actual fact in the greatest variety but
good judgement, sound logic and deep emotional drive.
It helps us to understand the greatness of Lowes'
scholarship to remember that, when he undertook this
work, he had become an authority on Chaucer, all
that pertained to him, to his works, and to the Middle
Ages.[7] This of itself formed a foundation of erudition
and insight of a sort rarely brought to bear on the
study of any modern author. One should add that in
his work on Chaucer there is none of the narrowness
of specialization. If the mastery of the particular is
the basis of broad and effective knowledge, as it is,
there is no better example than *The Road to Xanadu*.

The chaos that Lowes turns into cosmos is the great
but seemingly disorderly mind of Coleridge. If any
reader is uncertain about the existence and nature of
William James' stream of consciousness or the four-
dimensional space-time continuum, let him read this
book and also the voluminous Notes, and he will
know how the total human environment records iself
in the human brain. He will see, however, that the
mind of Lowes, as well as that of Coleridge, proceeds
in its operations by means of actualities. For example,
Lowes makes continual and effective use of the so-
called Gutch Memorandum Book, itself so cryptic and
fragmentary that nothing short of the widest and
most patient erudition plus the training of a scholar
could have understood it. Lowes' psychology, of which
of course there is a constant use, is correct but un-

technical. He uses freely, as we all do, the terminology of faculty psychology, most frequently of course in the word 'imagination', which is the stock-in-trade of Wordsworth and Coleridge. One fears at times that Lowes will yield to the temptation to make of imagination a sort of superior intelligence, but he escapes and knows what he is doing. He uses freely the words 'mind' and 'brain' and other designations of the intellect. For example, in one place he says casually,[8] 'But I have long had the feeling, which this study has matured to a conviction, that Fancy and Imagination are not two persons at all, but one.' There is little or no trace in the book of the relativistic concept of cognition, but Lowes' invincible and trained common sense causes him to say nothing that contradicts that naturalistic theory. The nearest he comes to the modern concept is his recognition of the truth of the method (axiomatic in origin) of the French mathematician Henri Poincaré. Lowes quotes at some length from *Science et Méthode*,[9] and the quotations include these statements, certainly illustrative of Lowes' own experience in the mastery of truth. Poincaré is discussing 'these appearances of sudden illumination, [which are] obvious indications of a long course of previous unconscious work', and he proceeds, 'This unconscious work . . . is not possible, or in any case not fruitful, *unless it is first preceded and then followed by a period of conscious work.*' Also:

All that we can hope from these inspirations, which are the fruits of unconscious work, is to obtain points of departure for [our] calculations. As for the calculations themselves, *they must be made in the second period of conscious work which follows the inspiration. . . . They demand discipline, attention, will, and consequently consciousness.* In the subliminal ego, on the contrary, there reigns what I would call liberty, if one could give the name to the mere absence of discipline and to disorder born of chance. Only, this very disorder permits of unexpected couplings.

It is no small tribute to Lowes' distinguished intelligence that he should see the bearings of Poincaré's mathematical speculations on his own problem. In his last chapter, 'Imagination Creatrix', a chapter that draws near in essence to the idea of the space-time four-dimensional continuum, Lowes recurs significantly to Poincaré. He is speaking of the climax of Darwin's great discovery and of the long, slow storing of the 'Well', of the 'flash of amazing vision', and of the exacting task of translating the vision into its actuality. He adds:

And these are essentially the stages which Poincaré observed and graphically recorded in his 'Mathematical Discovery'. And that chapter reads, as we saw long ago, like an exposition of the creative processes through which 'The Ancient Mariner' came to be. . . . It is of the utmost moment to more than poetry that instead of regarding the imagination as a bright but ineffective faculty with which in some esoteric fashion poets and their kind are specially endowed, we recognize the essential oneness of its function and its ways with all the creative endeavours through which human brains, with dogged persistence, strive to discover and realize order in a chaotic world.

This practically settles the matter. The word 'imagination' is still used, but it is no longer supernatural in its significance.

Lowes' repeated use of the metaphor of the 'Well' is also worth considering. He derived it from Henry James, who remarks that he took the original suggestion for the plot of *The American* and 'dropped it for the time into the deep well of unconscious cerebration'.[10] Lowes adopted it perhaps because he saw the need in mental activity of what Plato called The Receptacle. As a figure of speech, it is perhaps too static to serve as well as does the Receptacle and is certainly less appropriate to the activities of the mind than is the four-dimensional space-time continuum as conceived of by relativistic philosophers. It is only fair to say, however, that Lowes provides for activity in his 'well', so that it becomes, not a mere storage basin, but a workshop of the mind. The field of the subconscious or unconscious is full of pitfalls and they ought to be cleared out. Lowes does well enough in avoiding these hazards, but one rejoices that he did not complicate his task with the theories of Freud.

In fact Lowes is not guided and restrained by theories, and my contention is that his broad knowledge and his ability as a scholar to recognize truth in his researches in the realm of the particular, brings it about that his work really anticipates the space-time four-dimensional continuum and operates vigorously and correctly without the theory. He thus anticipates and illustrates the as yet unknown relativistic theory of cognition. This is as it should be. Thought must be an actual entity and a natural process. No one can so far explain what goes on in the process of thought or cognition, which is unintelligible, and the best that can be done to make clear its status as an actual automatic activity is to examine its basis in detail and see how a great scholar collected materials of operation. Lowes thus escapes the ancient and still current error of resorting to mysticism or divine intervention to account for the works of genius under his inspection. We do not know enough, however, to be sure that the space-time continuum is merely chaos, although it may seem to us in its variety to be heterogeneous, but its possible arrangement and order we do not know. In fact it is clear from Lowes' own work that Coleridge himself with his strange temperament—his zeal, his memory, his numerous impossible aspirations, and his high artistic and aesthetic passion—was building for himself his own space-time continuum, which through his marvellous mind may have had an order that we do not understand.

Lowes himself says:

The web of creation, like the skein of life, is a mingled yarn, conscious and unconscious inextricably intertwined. We are bound to *distinguish* (if we are ever to understand) between the constituents of any state or process worthy to be called a whole. We *divide* at the cost of our saving hold on integrality. The caution is Coleridge's, not mine; and imaginative reactions, if we have learned anything at all from the strange phantasmagoria which we are studying, is one process, and not two.[11]

This statement is in immediate agreement with the new theory of cognition which in its turn is regarded as one process and not two. It leaves no room either for angels of revelation, superhuman powers, or such intermediary agents as the faculties of the older psychology.

This also suggests something exemplified in Lowes' procedure. In accordance with a simple concept of the operation of thought, it must follow that the materials of cognition are necessarily entities in the environment. In Lowes' study of the genesis of 'The Ancient Mariner', Coleridge's use of the concrete actual is demonstrable to the last degree, and one is suddenly aware that this is the very essence of Shakespeare's art, who invents no plots and seems to have regarded events as God's affair. His was the task of expression and interpretation. When one looks about, one sees that the environment—factual , and emotional or romantic—

was also the very substance of Chaucer's thought and expression. Milton was so widely read and so aware of the world that he seems almost omniscient. The same thing seems also to be true of the greatest authors. One may say this at least that the greatest poets act like human rather than supernatural beings. One finds this principle expressed by Poe, one of the profoundest of critics. In *Peter Snook*[12] he flies in the face of tradition when he says, 'to originate is carefully, patiently, and understandingly to combine'. And one finds Lowes proceeding on the belief that the power of thought is to combine, or, as he says, 'integrate'. He speaks of it as 'the architectonic imagination'. He says indeed that the imagination never acts in a vacuum.[13]

Let us carry the idea of actuality into Lowes' perspicacious account of the structural features of 'The Ancient Mariner', not forgetting as we do so, the high romantic interest of Coleridge and his early contemporaries in voyages, travels and books about strange and unknown lands and seas.

Near the end of Chapter XIII Lowes says, 'For "the Rime of the Ancient Mariner" is a work of pure imagination, and Coleridge has so referred to it.' He does not, however, let that statement stand, but continues:

And this study, far from undermining that declaration, is lending it confirmation at every turn. For a work of pure imagination is not something fabricated by a *tour de force* from nothing, and suspended, without anchorage in fact, in the impalpable ether of a visionary world. No conception could run more sharply counter to the truth.[14]

And he says again,

For 'the images [which] rose up before him as things' rose up from somewhere. And our study of 'The Ancient Mariner' has revealed the fact that Coleridge's memory was tenanted by throngs of visual images from books.

Again in another place,

The imagination which may and does strike to the centre of what is universally valid in experience without passing across the threshold of the straitest hut, may also draw no less triumphantly within the compass of that same experience, for incorporation with it, the multifarious riches of the four corners of the earth. And one of the touchstones of supreme imaginative vision lies in its unerring recognition of what is universal in the remote and strange.

We do not know and may never know the details of the cognitive process, but, as Lowes himself sees, studies of this kind enable us to understand from its effects certain main features of cognition and to gain an idea of its unaided powers. The last sentence of the statement just quoted suggests a principle worth recording, namely, the amplification of the possibilities of ideation. Lowes has just quoted a passage from Thomas Maurice's *Memoir of a Map of Hindoostan* or the 'valley or country of Cashmere', which had suggested certain lines and images in *Kubla Khan*, and he says,

There are links in plenty to catch up Major Rennell's picture into that stream of images which were rising before the sleeping Coleridge as *things*—the miraculous fountains, and the fertile ground, and the river that opened a passage through the mountains, and the sunny garden spot. And the landscape of the deep romantic vale of Cashmere and the landscape of the valley of the upper Nile seem to have melted into one another in the dream, and the enchanted territory of the poem becomes '*holy land*'.[15]

This is not only important for its idea of blending, or combining, but it also suggests, as many other citations in the book from voyagers and travellers do, the necessity of expanding the range of knowledge felt by many writers and thinkers during the period in which Coleridge lived. It tends to make of the Romantic Movement a renascence. A reaching out for new ideas and greater knowledge seems to be a primary characteristic of all such rebirths.

It is interesting to observe that *The Road to Xanadu* is thought of as criticism by the critics and as scholarship by the scholars, and it is just these two things in one. It is therefore the best illustration I know of a modern work that refuses to commit the unnatural act of separating fact from its interpretation.

In the same year, 1926, in which Professor Broad's *The Philosophy of Francis Bacon* appeared there was published also *Science and the Modern World* by the late Professor A. N. Whitehead.[16] It is not and could not be at that time a fully developed treatise on the epistemology of the relativistic philosophy, but it is sound as far as it goes and will serve our purpose. It can be easily supplemented by Whitehead's later works and by those of Samuel Alexander, Lord Russell and various others.[17] The small work is conservative in its approach, but it does bring up the question of whether the relativistic philosophy of Einstein and his followers applies to all knowledge whatsoever or only to knowledge of the physical sciences. I am not able to pass on this, but I can see that an affirmative answer to the question is of the greatest importance to the future of literature and other discursive subjects. In fact I see in it, as the following chapters will show, a new freedom and a new direction with the possibility of progress.

Science and the Modern World is a hopeful book. It contains masterly sketches of the progress of science in the seventeenth, eighteenth and nineteenth centuries. The seventeenth century is treated as 'the Century of

Genius', and is, in my experience, unequalled in its perspicacity. With the seventh chapter he comes to Relativity, and his operation becomes less certain and his prose more difficult. But it is evident that relativity introduces a new element into the philosophy of science. This is well known and need not be explained here. Following this is a chapter on the Quantum Theory, which is carried through in rather difficult terms. The question posed by this doctrine is that of an actual break, if not a contradiction, in the course of scientific truth. Dr. James B. Conant, for example, in *Modern Science and the Modern Man*[18] finds a point beyond human comprehension in the fact that light manifests itself both as a wave phenomenon and a corpuscular phenomenon ('like a stream of bullets', he says). The quantum theory, so far as we know, does not concern us. But any break in the positivism of science has an interest of its own. We may also pass over the chapter on Science and Philosophy, which should, however, be combined with Lord Russell's essay, 'On Scientific Method in Philosophy' (1914). Chapter X, entitled Abstraction, certainly concerns the whole field of mental life, but Whitehead's treatment of the subject is so technical as to be far away from immediate understanding, and it is perhaps better to consider the subject in the simpler terms of Mrs. Susanne Langer's *An Introduction to Symbolic Logic*[19] (Second Edition (revised). New York, 1953). Even there we need go no further than Chapters IV (Generalization) and the succeeding chapters, which deal with Classes. In this subject is the possibility of finding a logical instrument that will serve the needs of discursive subjects, for it is certainly true in every area in which truth resides that the context of every generalization, that is the concepts on which it is based, should agree in their intension or meaning and be as complete as possible in extension or total membership.

The matter may be taken for granted, but so far there is no hint that truth was to be determined anywhere except in science. But at this point, as if in answer to prayer, comes a chapter in Whitehead's book on God. God is certainly a case in point. He is not like a mineral whose nature can be determined by chemical analysis, either qualitative or quantitative. The immediate interest is this and the remaining chapters of *Science and the Modern World*—'Religion and Science' and 'Requisites for Social Progress'—is in the fact that they appear and in the fact that their procedure is not in the narrow sense scientific. They are honest and skilful attempts to arrive at truth by means of correct abstraction. They therefore leave the door to the chamber of truth ajar for all comers.

The method of the chapter on God will be suggested by the following excerpts: [20]

In the place of Aristotle's God as Prime Mover, we require God as the Principle of Concretion. . . . We conceive of actuality as in essential relations to an unfathomable possibility. Eternal objects inform actual occasions with hierarchic patterns, included and excluded in every variety of discrimination.

It is important for my argument to insist upon the unbounded freedom within which the actual is a unique categorical determinant.

According to this argument the fact that there is a process of actual occasions, and the fact that the occasions are the emergence of values which require such limitation, both require that the course of events should have developed amid an antecedent limitation composed of conditions, particularization, and standards of value.

God is not concrete, but He is the ground for concrete actuality. No reason can be given for the nature of God, because that nature is the ground of rationality.

If He be conceived as the supreme ground for limitation, it stands in His very nature to divide the Good from the Evil, and to establish Reason 'within her dominions supreme'.

This is a mere fragment, but it may suggest a search for truth in another manner than that of controlled experiment. The chapter on Religion and Science affords still better examples, as the following will suggest: [21]

When we consider what religion is for mankind, and what science is, it is no exaggeration to say that the future course of history depends upon the decision of this generation as to the relation between them.

He then suggests that a broader field of reference (like a large-scale map) will serve to dissipate or reconcile seeming contradictions between religion and science, for—

In both regions of thought, additions, distinctions, and modifications have been introduced.
Remember the widely different aspects of events which are dealt with in science and in religion respectively.

For

The clash is a sign that there are wider truths and finer perspectives within which a reconciliation of a deeper religion and a more subtle science will be found.

One pauses to ask whether these truths are axiomatic or derived from patient observation resulting in a total view. The answer is possibly to be found in this sentence:

So far, my point has been this: that religion is the expression of one type of fundamental experiences of mankind: that religious thought develops into an increasing accuracy of expression, disengaged from adventitious imagery: that the interaction between religion and science is one great factor in promoting this development.

3

Religion has emerged into human experience mixed with the crudest fancies of barbaric imagination. Gradually, slowly, steadily the vision recurs in history under nobler form and clearer expression. . . . Apart from it, human life is a flash of occasional enjoyment lighting up a mass of pain and misery, a bagatelle of transient experience.

'Evil,' says Whitehead, 'is the brute motive force of fragmentary purpose, disregarding the eternal vision.'

Two citations from the thirteenth chapter are also well worth making.[22] In the first, Whitehead is discussing what we should call specialization in discursive fields:

Now to be mentally in a groove is to live in contemplating a given set of abstractions. The groove prevents straying across country, and the abstraction abstracts from something to which no further attention is paid. But there is no groove of abstractions which is adequate for the comprehension of human life.

The second, also worth noting by way of confirmation, is this:

The general conceptions introduced by science into modern thought cannot be separated from the philosophical situation as expressed by Descartes. I mean the assumption of bodies and minds as independent individual substances, each existing in its own right apart from any necessary reference to each other.

These chapters seem to show Whitehead making with great skill generalizations on a high level from abstractions that he believes to be sound, and why not? He is noted for this very thing.

About the end of the first quarter of this century there were thus issued three serious works which are discriminable in method. There was that of the self-respecting scientist who, without prejudice to other kinds of possible truth, refused to proceed one step beyond what he regarded as established scientific truth. This seems to have been the point of view of Professor C. D. Broad in *The Philosophy of Francis Bacon.*

There was also what was described as the practice of great scholars, and this search for truth was illustrated at some length from *The Road to Xanadu* by the late Professor John Livingston Lowes. This seemed to mean exact observation of particulars and their actual interrelations and, without *a priori* theory, the formulation of concepts that are simply and merely in line with facts. These facts need not be merely events or occurrences but may be drawn from any level of thought, emotion or artistry. What more does one want? Certainly not the close bounds of experimental science, which, although magnificently effective in experimental fields of learning, is at best only partly applicable in discursive fields. In fact, in the continuum with which we are concerned, error may reach a vanishing point. True scholarship needs and often has the determined spirit of science and will be satisfied with nothing less than truth, but the scientific method breaks down more and more in discursive fields.

It is easy but unintelligent to say that there is no such thing as truth except by way of scientific demonstration, for there is another older way that has been the basis of the evolution of culture. This is by means of the human brain, and with the mighty achievements of humanity in other fields than natural science before us, it is absurd either to deny its truth or to be completely non-committal about it. Great and useful attempts have been made to bridge the gulf between tangible and intangible truth by logical and epistemological studies of probability, but, important, indeed necessary, as those studies are, they seem to be supplementary to experimental science and do not take their origin from discursive subjects themselves.

That there is truth in these intangible subjects can be argued from effect to cause, and the history of civilization is a witness that there is truth in religion, philosophy, the social sciences and the humanities. This seems to be a sensible argument, although it is admittedly vague. There is, however, a basal concept to be seen in Lord Russell's famous question: If the axioms of mathematics are to be accepted as true, why may not self-evident truths in other fields be also accepted as true? Whether the answer to this is affirmative or not, it will have to be our working basis because we have no other. We in our age are, however, no more helpless than have been our ancestors. We can, as they did, fall in behind those who have possessed sane, intelligent and active minds, and although our difficulties may be greater than those of persons who can use mathematics and controlled experiment, we need not despair.

This is the reason such stress has been put in this chapter on scholarship, in which, in my judgment, is to be included actual criticism. If the natural powers and methods of scholarship are our main reliance, it is obvious that we must have an open field. The partitions, obstructions, theories and dogmatisms that we have created for ourselves or have adopted from others must be cleared away. This may be an impossibility. Certainly it is the most difficult thing we in the discursive fields have to do. Some part of the rest of this book will be devoted, reluctantly but necessarily, to the identification of these hindrances to progress.

In the third place, we have gathered from A. N. Whitehead's *Science and the Modern World* some of the rudiments of a new epistemology which seems in its naturalism to be the philosophy of true scholarship. We believe that the epistemology that has grown and is growing out of the philosophy of relativism offers us in the humanities a promise of improvement by rendering more consciously effective the best things we now do.

CHAPTER II

ENCLOSED AREAS

> I agree with Bergson's protest [against the intellectual
> spatialization of things], but I do not agree that such
> distortion is a vice necessary to the intellectual appre-
> hension of nature. . . . There is an error; but it is
> merely the accidental error of mistaking the abstract
> for the concrete. It is an example of what I will call
> the 'Fallacy of Misplaced Concreteness'. This fallacy
> is the occasion of great confusion in philosophy.—
> Whitehead, *Science and the Modern World*.

IN THE study of literature, as in the study of nature
or of life itself, we are confronted with the necessity
of examining and comprehending a vast body of
particulars in a field of unlimited extent and infinite
variety. We may see, to begin with, that any method
that narrows the field is productive of error. This approach is not, as it is often thought to be, a mere matter
of choice between an *a priori* and an *a posteriori* procedure, since deduction and induction are not contra-
dictory the one to the other but are integrated and
concomitant. Nor must we resort hastily to the establishment and recognition of partitions between fields
of learning.

The details of the space-time continuum are so inter-
related that such partitions always do harm and can
be justified only on grounds of sheer quantity and
social necessity. The new epistemology reveals a gigantic accident (in the logical sense) that serves to mark
a distinction that arises from degree of manipulability.

It may be roughly stated thus: when controlled experiment is practicable, we have to do with science;
when it is impracticable or impossible, we have to do
with discursive subjects—religion, philosophy, large
parts of the social sciences and the humanities. It is
not of course a sharp line, but it is sufficient to send
us, as it sent our ancestors, into the wide field of human
life and its environment with no help but observation
and no hope but the achievement of ultimate wisdom.
This presupposes the unity of all knowledge to this
extent at least, namely, that the truth of fact is omnipresent and, I believe, achievable. For this most difficult of all intellectual undertakings the learning of
our time has provided a theory of cognition that shows
how it comes about and the conception of an instrument suited to the task so natural and so plausible
that there have been none to reject it. I refer again
to our vast neural complex whose function, no doubt
evolutionary in its origin, is to apprehend, comprehend, respond to and record the impact of the environment on the individual, the group and the race, to
which is fitted a process of cognition—recognition, abstraction and reaction taking place in the fourth
dimension.

We return to the essential idea that truth is one,
and the suggestion on that basis is that we accord our
search for reality with the process of attaining intellectual satisfaction,[1] or, to state this more simply, we
need to apply to the study of our subject an epistemology suited to its complexity and its complete comprehension. If this new metaphysics is a true metaphysics,
it concerns us in the most intimate way, since it provides us with the two things we need most: breadth
or universality of vision and freedom. It may be, as we
shall see, that it suggests the possibility of renascence.

It also changes our attitude towards the discovery of truth from positivism to relativity. This also we shall need to take up later.

As said above, the process of cognition has always been a mystery, and that mystery, now dispelled, has been the mother of superstition and a fountain of error. Because men did not understand the enormous capabilities of the human mind and were ignorant of its processes, they resorted to divine intervention either direct or in the form of a superhuman faculty called intuition in order to explain achievements beyond the range of their immediate comprehension. The new epistemology simply fills the gap and leaves no need or room for supernaturalism and seems to show that man is capable of works of genius whether he thinks so or not. It provides a conception of Deity so noble that it despises hocus-pocus and freakish favouritism. The older mystical view lives and flourishes still; not even Bergson and Croce are entirely free from the traditional bonds. Some literary critics and many minor poets are still defending what one hopes is the last redoubt of superstition. They call it the organic theory of art and think of themselves as possessed by a god (ἐνθουσιασμόι).

The new theory of cognition, with its base in a sort of Platonic receptacle called the space-time continuum, provides for an equitable coexistence and interaction of induction and deduction, which are ancient and natural participants in the discovery of truth. The Elizabethans, being fortunately for them Pre-Cartesian, were not hampered and restrained as we are by *a priori* dogmatism in the use of their minds. But their freedom was not to be inherited by their literary successors. Critics and literary men took over the edicts of the scientific method and let dogmatism determine the rules and subjects of their activity; indeed let themselves be classified. In our field at this time, indeed particularly since the late nineteenth century, deduction, often in disregard of the ontological principle, has been overstressed and our subject fragmented and warped from its true nature and function.

I myself remember the invasion of American universities by the scientific method applied to literature, history and other discursive subjects. I was taught by two different kinds of university teachers: the one made up of wise, kindly and sincere students of literature who had, most of them, been trained in the principles of the Scottish school of philosophy in what was called Baconian induction. In fact they knew no other method of procedure except knowledge, experience and honest human judgement. The invasion by the proponents of the scientific method was as a *Blitzkrieg*. The air was full of such words as *These, Fach, Seminar, die Methode* and *die Doktorwürde*. Their victory was complete, and the inductionists retired in defeat, carrying with them a humiliating sense of their own inferiority. Yet, allowance being made for cultural conditions and lack of opportunity, these defeated men were more nearly right and were actually more effective as teachers and interpreters of literature and as promoters of creative efforts than were their conquerors.

An unnecessary formalism deductively applied is the worst possible thing for progress in discursive subjects, and it has become universal. Such subjects cannot be sliced into periods and particularized forms. We cannot by the very nature of our quest for truth afford specialization in the parts of parts, and the consequences are now being felt in our lack of progress. To be just about it, indispensable things were accom-

plished, mainly of course in the factual areas of our
field, by the scientific group—dictionaries, epitomes,
biographies, bibliographies, and such aids to study as
the accumulation of materials, the publication of texts,
and, for a time at least, the perfection of historiographical techniques: Our subject took on a different
kind of interest and lost much of its natural appeal,
as if there were nobody left to read and write books,
enjoy them and think about them. Indeed, we have
developed a hostility to new ideas in as stiff a body of
dogmatists as exist in the world today. One rubs one's
eyes and says, 'But this is English language and literature, the record of our race and the medium of our
thought!'

The authorities on these great subjects have acted
as if the brain were spatially limited and have thought
absurdly that a man can know only one thing and
that other things take up needed room in the human
head. Obviously they forget or never knew the estimate
of nine thousand million possibilities of ideation in
the human brain. We are overwhelmed with unsupported theories and treated as public enemies if we
call these theories in question. We, in spite of our
learning, are non-participants in the thing we teach
and have forced a division between those, often ignorant and ill equipped, who practice creative writing
and those who think of themselves as scholars. The
subject is narrowed and stagnant, and one hopefully
suggests that the positivistic course we have pursued
with its narrowing features is coming to an end and
that now appears a new direction. There seems to be a
sort of quantum manifestation in the waves of scholarly enterprise.

We have before us the well-supported concept of a
space-time continuum in the human mind, something

corresponding to and reflective of environment, indeed to entities themselves, especially to the less obvious and those of broader significance. This is, as a prospect, the broadest and most natural foundation on which the study and practice of literature has ever rested. It seems perfect in its promise of freedom, bristling with new tasks and new values and in line with creativity. It might unite literature with the study of literature, break down the false partition between scholarship and criticism and make authorship the function of the people. Why was it so in the age of Queen Elizabeth I and why is it not so in the age of Queen Elizabeth II? All learning is one. The physical sciences without knowing it have revealed this great truth, and, if we have the intelligence and zeal to follow this lead, it is not too much to say that, in spite of our selfish indulgence, our absorption in commerce and our dependence on the amusement business, we might yet start a great and lasting movement in life and art. Our people are static spectators, non-participants. Their wasteful frivolity and inordinate greed of gain are no new things in the world, and they live as they do largely because they are barred by dogmatism from any other life.

Nothing much can be done about this at once, but it would seem to be a simple duty to subject this intellectual situation to study and thought, which in the elapse of time may not be futile. The field of examination is the relation between conventions and widely held opinions, whether inherited or newly invented, and the actualities of literature and life. The obvious principle is that generalizations have no value, indeed are harmful in various ways, unless they are based on fact. The rest of this chapter will be devoted to the illustration of this principle, in order to show that

absorption in false or only partly true so-called principles without constant recourse to actual fact produces
stagnation and is deadly to true scholarship. In other
words, positivism should not be carried into areas that
are by their very nature relativistic. Our goal, let me
say, is far more concrete and hopeful than this sounds.

Our primary concern is with the field of the humanities. There we find a very ancient and important
general theory that concerns us, that of forms and
kinds.

In 1916 there appeared an article of some length by
Roy Kenneth Hack entitled 'The Doctrine of Literary
Forms'.[2] It was ahead of its time and met with hostility or indifference among classical scholars. It will
nevertheless serve to bring before us a general conflict
between a narrower and a broader concept of literature
and its nature and function. It has to do with the doctrine of literary forms derived from Plato and Aristotle, which has had almost overwhelming influence
from the time of its origin until now. The author of
this article contended that Plato's stern adherence to
truth as he saw it served to rule out freedom of action
in literary composition and thus forbade the variation
that belongs to the individual and to his environment.
Aristotle in the doctrine of mimesis gave currency,
authority and practicality to Plato's doctrine.

It might be well to let the author of this article tell
his own story. He begins with a study of *Ars Poetica*
by Horace and shows that Horace repeats Aristotle's
principles as embodied in the *Poetics* and put forward
as laws and, particularly, that Greek meters, as brought
over into Latin poetry, were definitely required by
the kinds of poetry to which they had been assigned.
He discovered that Horace, though completely faithful
to Aristotelian dicta, did not in his own practice adhere

to them. Personal and individual matters are intruded rather freely into metrical forms to which according to rule they do not belong. This is regarded as evidence that these forms are not absolute in nature and that their tendency is to restrict a freedom called for by human environment. The following paragraph will make clear the earlier part of the contention:

We began with an examination of the doctrine of literary forms as it has been applied to the criticism of the *Ars Poetica*; we discovered that it produced confusion and disagreement; we then studied the doctrine as promulgated by Horace and found that it did not avail to explain his own poetry. We then undertook to trace the genealogy of this doctrine and its corollary, the doctrine of propriety; and we learn from Cicero not only that they permeate his rhetorical writings but also that they have been borrowed from Plato. We have already given serious grounds for the belief that the doctrine of literary forms is not sound. So far as critics trust themselves to it, they are betrayed into externality, into prolonged examination of the outer features and into wrangling over classifications; while the individual and personal, the heart and soul of the truth, are left severely alone, or are dismissed briefly as mere aesthetic trifles. Is it conceivable that Plato is responsible for this erroneous method of literary criticism? Has Cicero any justification for attributing his scheme of eloquence to the great philosopher?

I believe that Cicero is right, and that Plato is responsible.

The following[3] will make the position still clearer and possibly pave the way to a deeper understanding of our own situation, in which, however, the contrasting ideas are not exactly the same, but may be analogous:

The laws of nature are unalterable; in so far as we have to do with them, we are in unqualified subjection to them. When we speak of man's conquest of nature, we do not mean that these laws have been transformed by man, but merely that increasing knowledge of them has enabled us to avail ourselves of principles imperfectly known hitherto. Science lays down rules that man must obey; and strict obedience to these rules is a guarantee of perfect success, or rather of success which is perfect within certain limits and in certain ways. To forget the limitations of science is literally a fatal error, an error that brings death with it; for it does away with and utterly destroys (in logic, though not in fact) the creative activity of man. Nothing can be more sure than that science and scientific method do not and cannot govern the whole of human life; man is not always in subjection to scientific rules, and he actually does a great deal for which no rules can be given. This other side of human life is the creative, the poetic activity of man. Without this side, man would have no history, and the world would be a mere mechanism; but inasmuch as he possesses it, he is not bound but free, so that he can achieve, create, invent. His creative power is of course limited, precisely as science is limited. They are in fact two reciprocal functions; neither one can dispense with the other. The scientist cannot do without the poetic faculty, any more than the poet can afford to disregard the law of gravitation.

With the general position here explained there is little fault to be found. There is no poetic faculty that is the exclusive possession of poets. There is merely a continuum of imaginative creativity and appreciation in human nature that increases from the merest trace to the highest known perfection, and it is to be noted that the author subsumes under this too-narrow term the whole area of human life not subject to scientific determination. He is in general right, but what he lacks in the concept with which this book begins, namely, that so-called discursive subjects do not yield to the experimentation and demonstration of verifiable truth. The author sees the actuality and importance of such experiential subjects and lays the basis for the contention that literature, if it is to reflect the truth, beauty and goodness of human life and its environment, must be free from formal limitation. From another point of view, that is the history of the slow unfolding of truth about man's total environment, I am not only willing to forgive Plato but to believe that his perception of the role of truth in poetry was a salutary step in behalf of order. It is not meant for impertinence when I say that it is a pity that neither Plato nor Aristotle saw consciously that one truth appears throughout the environment, both factual and ratiocinative. That they both knew these values needs no argument. Socrates was a very source of wisdom, and Aristotle an authority on the whole range of learning.

Hack's charge against Plato, much of which must be borne by Plato's followers, is expressed in these terms:

This error of Plato's was rapidly transformed into a definite system of aesthetics and of criticism; and it has profoundly influenced all men and all things which have since come into contact with it, be they little or great, Horace or Aristotle, the Alexandrian grammarians or the mediaeval scholastics, Scaliger, Boileau, Pope, or Taine, Brunetière and Norden.

And this by way of further clarification:

Since scientific truth is also (for Plato) moral perfection and since gods and heroes are morally perfect, a poet who represents gods and heroes as immoral beings is irreverent, offensive and injurious; that is, he violates propriety inasmuch as he is false to the perfect form. The poet must be compelled to impress upon his poems the likeness of moral perfection; failing in that, he fails in all.

We may stop at this point, since the matter at issue is in its simple outlines clear. All of us would probably admit that it is true that Aristotle or pseudo-Aristotle and other forms of neo-classicism have restrained exuberance and variety in literary creation and that this author is right as regards the facts of his opinion. But there have always been those who regarded restraint as a necessity of art, and in the controversy over classicism and romanticism have preferred the former.[4] With reference to Aristotle himself and still more to Plato there is always the question of whether or not they have been correctly understood and interpreted. The important work of S. H. Butcher in England and Lane Cooper in the United States went a long way in giving the modern world a correct idea of Aristotle and his teachings about poetry and drama, and Aristotle emerged in broader and more generally significant terms than he had ever before.[5] It has seemed to me that Aristotle is not by any means a dogmatist and that he examined the literature of his age and country with the broad and true vision of a good scholar and scientist. It is possibly unfair to interpret him as laying down laws for authors and critics rather than as one who simply understood and explained what he saw. Aristotle, being a great scholar, was certainly not so positivistic as he has been thought to have been. It is possibly absurd to carry modern controversies so far back into the ancient world. About the *Ars Poetica* there can be little doubt that it is an intelligent and positivistic manual of rules of poetic and dramatic literature.

My own approach has been from a different angle— a distrust of positivism in any such field or in any field of research whatever. I can understand the attitude and feelings of positivistic thinkers in our own time. They want matters settled and are proud of themselves for having found out and mastered certain structural and factual parts of eternal and unshakable truth.

They are rather pleased to think that Aristotle said, 'Let there be poetry of these kinds: pastoral, elegiac, iambic, comic and tragic,' just as God said, 'Let there be a firmament in the midst of the waters, and let it divide the waters from the waters.' But it seems that a positivistically perfect literary structure cannot be built. It must be said that Aristotle's thought was on a high level of abstraction and was so soundly conceived as to Greek poetry that it has and has had bearing on all poetic criticism. But, in the infinite variety of human life and its issues, it was too much to expect that he would be able to legislate for all time, all ages and all races. The relativistic point of view makes this clear and also makes it obvious that his inferior successors have no choice but to operate broadly and accurately within the bounds of truth as he did.

The conditions round about the search for truth have undergone some changes. Classification is a matter of greater uncertainty and less importance than it has been thought to be, and it is a commonplace that such labels as lyric and epic, if understood in traditional senses do not fit the packages to which they are attached. This is the case even in the famous genre tragedy, and some discussion of that concept will appear further on in this book. How seriously we are in need of a new poetic morphology I do not know, nor what the criteria of such a context might be. I can see the necessity of concretion, but I do not know who is to make it. Great scholars are the highest hope, for they would know literature, but it is possible that they would need, for complete success, to know philosophy. Philosophers, in spite of their protests, are specialists—in philosophy—and may not know literature.

But the world of literary criticism, like large areas

4

of current thought in many fields, is full of a variety
of opinions and generalizations that are not so soundly
based on actual data as were the doctrines of Aristotle
and therefore not so durable. The best of them are
possibly authoritative and are true in proportion to
the soundness of the authority. Many of their speculations, however, are mere guesses or stupid primary conclusions with or without concretion and living on
because of thoughtless positivistic repetition. They
become merely a way of talking, thought of, if subject
to thought at all, as concrete, indeed mistaken for the
concrete. Whitehead, who has little to say about literature, has shown the necessity of basing all generalizations on actual fact. He calls it 'concrescence' and regards it as the simplest and most basal idea in the
whole process of thought when directed towards the
discovery of truth. It connects itself, indeed actually is,
the process of symbolization on which the growth of
mind, from infancy to old age, is based. In *Process and
Reality* Whitehead makes of it the fourth Category of
Explanation and describes it in these terms:

That the potentiality for being an element in a real
concrescence of many entities into one actuality, is the one
general metaphysical character attaching to all entities,
actual and non-actual. In other words, it belongs to the
nature of a 'being' that it is a potential for every 'becoming'. This is 'the principle of relativity'.

A great deal of space in this book and others by
Whitehead is devoted to the analysis of the function
of the concrete, and he arrives at a definition as
follows:

'Concrescence' is the name for the process in which the
universe of many things acquires an individual unity in
a determinate relegation of each item of the 'many' to its
subordination in the constitution of the novel 'one'.[6]

If the world of mind, lacking conclusions based on the actual, remained empty except for such established truths, Whitehead's description would be merely a careful and ingenious metaphysical study, which could be safely neglected. But it happens that our world is full to overflowing with generalizations—some sound, some partly true, some false, some drawn by false analogy from the outside, and some so vague as to have no meaning at all. Except the first, these things are not innocent. As a whole they spread and perpetuate falsehood. These imperfect or false 'concrescences' are mistaken for actual entities and thus operate in thought as fact. This is serious of course, but probably in the field of literature the greatest harm comes when this debased currency puts out of use literature itself in which alone value exists.

The principle of false concretion must apply very widely in the whole area of thought. For example, a very brilliant and effective use is made of it by C. S. Lewis in *The Screwtape Letters*, where it is satirically applied with a consistency that reminds one of Swift.[7] In letters to Wormwood, his nephew, Screwtape, an old and experienced devil, explains the techniques of winning souls away from God, religion and truth, as also the mistakes that may cause human beings to reject the devil. It is a mistake, Screwtape says, to resort to argument, which may lead the 'patient' to consider actual things in God's world and thus behold the truth, which in Screwtape's system is to be avoided at all costs. True reason, he says, no longer motivates man, who now prefers to deal in large and vague generalities. An appeal to reason might be fatal, for it would turn the mind of the patient (who is in danger of becoming a Christian) to great universal issues. One way to prevent this is to keep his mind on sensual indulgences; call them 'real life'. Science, he says, is mistakenly considered an enemy of religion. Not at all. Science will encourage the man to think of the intangible realities beyond the tangible ones. Don't let him get into sciences—or not beyond economics and sociology. If Wormwood cannot keep away from the subject, he must keep it general and talk with him about 'this modern scientific age'. The idea isn't to teach the patient, but to confuse him; keep it general. Give him a grand general idea that he knows it all and that everything he happens to have picked up in casual talk and reading is the result of 'modern investigation'. Further on Wormwood is instructed to this effect: 'It may even be the main attack, as long as he thinks it the subordinate one. But here, as in everything else, the way must be prepared for your moral assault by darkening his intellect.'

I should not know where to find any modern work from which by inversion so clear a picture of the evils of false and foolish thinking could be made. One is even tempted to transfer with appropriate changes the following statement to the field of literature: [8]

Cruel ages are put on their guard against Sentimentality, reckless and idle ones against Respectability, lecherous ones against Puritanism; and whenever all men are really hastening to be slaves or tyrants we make Liberalism the prime bogey.

But we need another defence against those who are wedded to outmoded ideas held with a dogmatism like that of Torquemada, although such dogmatic persons lack the executive opportunities of the inquisitor. They take it out in stupidity based on positivism and the laziness that it breeds. Clearly we need the *Epistolae Obscurorum Virorum*,[9] a work of the age of Reuchlin and Erasmus, all wisely anonymous. It lacks the subtlety of the *Screwtape Letters* but not the clarity of vision. It refers to a scholastic and not a religious state of mind.

The *Epistolae Obscurorum Virorum* arose from an immediate contest and controversy of the time. On one side were the humanist Johann Reuchlin and his friends and followers on the side of the new learning and the new Latin; on the other, Johann Pfefferkorn, an ambitious convert anxious for notoriety—on any terms. Pfefferkorn wrote a pamphlet against the Jews. Reuchlin replied in the spirit of humanistic tolerance and the controversy began. Jakob von Hoogstraten and the Predicants, the University of Cologne and the whole body of scholastics sided with Pfefferkorn. The leader chosen by the enemy was Gratius Ortovinus, a theologian of the established pattern at Deventer. The satire took the form of a long series of stupid, abusive, partisan letters in mostly bad Latin, letters in which sychophancy, ignorance and naïve self-revelation run riot. Behind them are the outworn and completely formalized doctrines of a completely dead scholasticism. The supposititious writers of the letters refer to realism and nominalism, Thomism and Scotism, but manifestly know nothing about them. The letters are full of scriptural quotations that have no application to the issues supposed to be under discussion, but are quoted at second-hand and for the ostentation of learning. The writers are naïve, but not innocently so, and thus reveal their own sensuality, idleness and selfish greed. They take an interest in academic degrees, ranks, promotions and jobs greater even than the modern world.

There is no comparison between the subtlety and refinement of C. S. Lewis's *The Screwtape Letters* and the crude, often brutal, satire of the *Epistolae Obscur-*

orum Virorum, but in one respect the two works fit together like hand and glove. Screwtape fights against the real. A 'patient' who comes into contact with God's actual world is lost to the kingdom of Hell. The vulgar, ignorant, idle boobies who write the fulsome letters to *Ortovinus Gratius Daventriensis poeta, Orator, et Philosophus, necnon theologus, et plus si vellet* are absolutely cut off from the real world and live in an artificial world of forms.

It is hard to find a selection from the letters of the Obscure Men that is subtle enough to be comparable to Lewis's book. Perhaps the letter of one Anton N., of the Art of Medicine almost a Doctor, in Letter XLII will serve. The point of the letter is contained in the words *tunc risit Erasmus et nihil respondit*:

Preceptor unparalleled! . . . As soon as I arrived hither, there came to me a good friend, and one very well-disposed towards me; you know him well, for he was for a long while under your ferule at *Cologne*—and he told me of a man named *Erasmus* of *Rotterdam*, of whom I had never heard, but who is profoundly skilled in all knowledge and in every branch of learning. This man, he told me was even then at *Strasburg* . . . Thereupon I earnestly begged my friend to bring me to *Erasmus* that I might see him. I had with me a note-book that I call my medical *Vade-mecum* . . . for I always carry it with me when I walk abroad to visit patients, or to buy simples— and in this are jotted down sundry very subtle questions concerning the medical art. Out of this note-book, therefore, I culled me a question with all the comments thereon, and the arguments *pro* and *con*, and armed with these I purposed to beset this man whom they deem so learned, and make trial whether he knew somewhat of Medicine, or not. Now when I told my friend my intent, he made a great feast, and bade to it speculative Theologians, and Jurists of high renown, and myself as a representative, all unworthy, of the Art Medicinal. . . .

At the last it was fairly brought to the proof, whether

that wiseacre was indeed a poet, as the report went. For as we all sat in silence, he began to hold forth in a mighty long preamble.

But of this—else I am no true-born man—I understood not a single word, by reason that he had such a wee little voice; I think he did in some sort handle theology, and this to engage a certain Magister Noster, a man of vast profundity in matters theological, who sat with us at board.

Thereupon, when *Erasmus* had concluded that prelude, the Magister Noster began to argue with great subtlety concerning entity and essence—but it skilleth not that I should recall his words, for you are well versed in such matters. When he had finished, *Erasmus* replied, but briefly, and once more we all sat silent. Our host, therefore, who is a humanist of parts, fell to some discourse on Poetry, and greatly belauded *Julius Caesar*, as touching both his writings and his valorous deeds. So soon as I heard this, I perceived my opportunity, for I had studied much, and learned much under you in the matter of Poetry, when I was at *Cologne,* and I said, 'Forasmuch as you have begun to speak concerning Poetry, I can therefore no longer hide my light under a bushel, and I roundly aver that I believe not that *Caesar* wrote those *Commentaries*, and I will prove my position with argument following, which runneth thus: Whosoever hath business with arms and is occupied in labour unceasing cannot learn Latin; but *Caesar* was ever at War and in labours manifold; therefore he could not become lettered and get Latin. In truth, therefore, I believe it was none other than *Suetonius* who wrote those *Commentaries*, for I have met with none who hath a style liker to *Caesar's* than *Suetonius*.'

After I had this spoken, and much else which here, for brevity's sake, I set not down—since, as you know from the ancient saw, 'The moderns delight in brevity'— *Erasmus* laughed, but said nothing, for I had overthrown him by the subtlety of my argument.

Heine has pointed academic satire that is, however, pleasant, but this is not the rule.[10] There is usually a savage intolerance in those who uphold the principles of a system whose falsity has been exposed, such as appears in the controversy that gave rise to the *Epistolae Obscurorum Virorum*. If anyone doubts this, let him read Aldous Huxley's *The Devils of Loudun*.

The fallacy of mistaking the abstract for the concrete, especially the pseudo-abtsract of ill-based propositions, will be referred to in later chapters of this book. Meantime, we may agree that a formal system of theories or sets of theories that neglects the actual and operates positivistically, in an area of mere opinion or tradition, narrows the field and is the enemy not only of truth but of progress.

It may be advisable to make clear by the study of an actual case the broad primarily inductive procedure necessary for the comprehension of those areas in discursive subjects that do not, and cannot, yield their full truth to an hypothetical approach; that is, an *a priori* method by means of the invention and argumentative proof of hypotheses. The difference is this: in deductive procedure the hypothesis comes first, or early in the investigation, whereas in the inductive method the solution or satisfaction comes last of all. In induction, demonstration in the scientific sense may be impossible, but higher and higher degrees of probability may be achieved, and questions at issue are kept open so that an ultimate wisdom may be secured. Let us take the case of Milton's *De Doctrina Christiana*.

In his noble and tolerant introduction addressed to 'All the Churches of Christ', Milton makes clear the details of his great inductive quest. It begins with himself and not with a pedantic pretence of instructing others:

I deem it therefore safest and most advisable to compile for myself, by my own labour and study, some original treatise which should be always at hand, derived solely from the word of God itself, and executed with all possible fidelity, seeing that I could have no wish to practise any imposition on myself in such a matter.

To achieve his purpose Milton will examine the Old and New Testaments verse by verse in order to determine what the Scriptures actually say and mean. An idea of his 'fidelity' may be seen in the seven thousand citations from the Bible, frequently with the text itself and with commentary.

Milton accepts Aristotle's treatment of ethics with its terminology, a thing he had a perfect right to do, but the concept of good and evil and the distinction between them is his own. It is therefore misrepresentative for Thomas Cuming Hall[11] and other writers on the history of ethics to dismiss Milton as merely a follower of Aristotle and Cicero, since, in point of fact, Milton reconstitutes the subject and sharpens its definitions throughout.

The first book, which is mainly theological, proceeds on a high metaphysical level in the treatment of God, His Providence, His Creation and His Rule or Government. The second book Milton devotes to the subject of human conduct, and there is in existence no work more carefully thought out in terms of actuality. In the eighth to the fourteenth chapter he makes his great contribution to practical ethics, which is possibly unequalled in the modern world. It lies in his distinction between the duties that a man owes to himself and those that he owes to his neighbour. He saw, in the first place, that without love and righteousness there is no human virtue possible. The great surprise comes, however, with Milton's enumeration of the duties that a man owes to himself—he had thought he owed them to his neighbours: temperance, sobriety, chastity, modesty, decency, contentment, frugality and industry. It follows that in these matters the man who says, 'I am holier than thou,' is merely saying, 'I am looking after myself better than thou art looking after thyself,' which is not a winsome thing to say. The duties that one owes to one's neighbours form a pleasant and unperplexing list, although, as Milton shows, these duties are on the borderland of the law. The docket of a general court will show what is involved.

One would grant that the history of a great race with its prophetic utterances would inevitably reveal the ethics of all races, as it does. What Milton accomplished by his patient clear-headed study was to arrive at a concept that has no need of scientific demonstration.

We, as students, can do little about the beliefs and trends of this brave new world, and our criticisms are not likely to be heeded. Let us therefore see if a freer resort to truth as it exists may not reveal a new direction and a new hope.

CHAPTER III

ETERNAL IDEAS

The Socratic dialectic only set itself to gain the art of
right thinking for the immediate use of individuals to
purify their crude presentations into concepts: the
practice of dialectic was therefore at the same time
education; intellectual and moral activity coincided,
as much for the work of the philosopher in itself as
for its effect on others. The Platonic dialectic, on the
other hand, was subservient to the formation of a
system: it has therefore, as compared with the Socratic, larger outlines and a more fixed form.—Jowett,
Dialogues of Plato.

PERHAPS IT would be agreed that intelligent
and sincere observation is a starting-point; indeed, it would be conceded that for us and our
subject, however it may be with scientists, experience
is the basis of comprehension. This becomes a special
and individual act since the stupid man or woman
sees only what he or she is told to look for; sees nothing or little for itself until something like interest or
purpose or concern enters and brings with it an emotional element. This drive becomes part of thought
itself.

One need not, however, speak so generally. The
record of what has been thought and felt and done we
call literature. It has, or may have, a value not only as
a record of the wisdom of the ages but as a pattern of
action. It takes on, as a construction of symbolization,
inevitably, although in varying degrees of adequacy, a

representation of forms. This was Plato's discovery, for he saw that the space-time continuum is not mere flux. If it were, nothing could be done with it. This determination of an organization may be said to be the basis of intelligibility, comprehension and the development of mind in the individual and of culture and civilization in the group.

The Renaissance is said to have come in and gone out with Plato, or rather Platonism, and it is here suggested that losses in the use and understanding of forms or eternal ideas have been and continue to be made in this area. It is not, however, merely the restoration of the doctrines of Plato, which might be restated in far greater correctness than they were in the Renaissance, that needs revival. They are still applicable and have in them the urge to renascence, but they need both supplementation and adjustment. Literature must be judged truly as a record as well as a construction, just as what is seen and heard and felt must be judged truly, and in all reason it must be experienced before it is judged. The actions and utterances of the past must be made a part of the present, and the process of bringing the past to life is the one with which the student of literature is concerned.

Before we consider the results of this process of translating the past into the present, it might be well to ask what it is that causes the past to come to life in the present and to do so in varying degrees of truth and vividness.

It is usually said in effect that the vitality of memory is a function of human nature and operates through the association of ideas, and this is no doubt true, but it remains vague. It may be that the intrusion of ideas of survival and of course great tendencies, motives and reactions into the complex itself would make our con-

cepts more definite. I know of no plausible theories
that furnish even a working basis and should like to
make a tentative suggestion as to why literature and
other forms of art live on with varying degrees of
vitality. To answer in terms of a mystical concept of
art seems superficial and inadequate. It may be that
this readiness of recall comes from deep and relatively
unchanging conditions of what human life has been
and continues to be, one may say roughly from needs,
tendencies and sentiments based on animal instincts
that live on in modified form in human beings and
constitute bases of emotion, motive and action. This
happens when the vital conditions of human existence
are appealed to by a record of fact brought by analogy
into the complex of the present. The field is broad and
the appeal varied but natural. One may not ignore the
necessity of breadth of knowledge, to gain it no easy
matter but yet in line with the task of scholarship,
which is the mastery of the particular. In general this
is the condition of renascence, and only the greatest
men in the greatest ages have been able to overcome
the obstacles that have stood in the way of progress.
Revival of the past may not be the only way in which
the human spirit can be revived, but it at least shows
that inanition is not a permanent state.

We need, however, some confirmation of the idea
that it is possible to operate logically on a theory that
within limits certain ideas and certain works embodying ideas do live on from age to age and readily appeal
to later times. Of course there can be no doubt that
they do. When psychologists speak of operations on
higher and higher levels of abstraction as produced by
increasing self-consciousness, they can hardly mean
self-consciousness as ordinarily defined and understood. Perhaps they mean what the Greeks meant by

'know thyself'. In other words, they must have in mind states and processes in the vast and vague class of universals or what Whitehead calls eternal ideas. If so, there is the possibility of some advance in understanding.[1]

Some advance has, indeed, been made in tracing a line of development from primitive instincts and sentiments into higher levels of generality. We cannot escape belief that trends of the most fundamental character can be perceived and partly traced from bottom to top in a series plainly within the concept of evolution from the most elementary to the most complex levels of abstraction. If this is true, humanity would be open to appeal by certain eternal ideas not only as a living race in the present but from age to age. Therefore with reference to bygone ages it is not enough to know their history. We must also hear their voices. When they give us signals, we must understand and react.

The tentative suggestion just made might be rendered more intelligible by a consideration of William McDougall's treatment of instincts, emotions, sentiments and abstractions on higher planes of thought as presented in *An Introduction to Social Psychology*.[2] This might open fields of thought as to why art and literature live on from generation to generation. He describes the nature of the instincts of man and follows this with an enumeration: the Instinct of Flight and the Emotion of Fear, the Instinct of Curiosity and the Emotion of Wonder, the Instinct of Pugnacity and the Emotion of Anger, the Instincts of Self-abasement and of Self-assertion and the Emotions of Subjection and Elation and the Parental Instinct and the Emotion of Tenderness. In a minor category he puts various other instincts with their emotions: instincts of reproduction, of gregariousness, of construction, and others. These constitute a primary list, and to them Mc-Dougall adds certain innate tendencies: Sympathy, Suggestion and Suggestibility, Imitation, Play and Temperament. He has also a chapter on Sentiments —with two lists. The first he calls Complex Emotions that do not necessarily imply the existence of Senti-ments: Admiration, Reverence, Gratitude, Scorn, Loathing and Envy. In the second are Complex Emo-tions that do imply the existence of Sentiments: Re-proach, Jealousy, Resentment and Shame. To this he adds consideration of Joy, Sorrow, Pity and Happi-ness. Sentiments, he says, undergo development appar-ently through the growth of Self-consciousness and the Self-regarding Sentiments. This is difficult to follow, but there is, at any rate, an Advance to the Higher Plane of Social Conduct, which would mean a higher level of abstraction. He has a chapter on Volition, which might be regarded primarily as a result of cog-nition. Finally, there is a long section in which the author applies his thought to the life of societies.

Unless I am very much mistaken, there is an idea in McDougall's work of more than casual importance. If there is, there seems to be a natural mental process, on the basis of psychology and human experience, of forming safe judgements on high levels of abstraction. It is possible that a natural epistemology applied to discursive subjects, together with a sound procedure according to the principles of symbolic logic, might produce at least high degrees of probability in fields still ignored or handled only from the point of view of faculty psychology. It concerns the discovery of truth and the basis of criticism, and I think we must resort to actual experience.

When I was a college student I began the study of

Odyssey with the rather gentle sixth book. Calipso had
sent Odysseus away on a raft, and he did well enough
until Poseidon saw him off the coast of Phaeacia and
wrecked his raft, but Odysseus got ashore and slept on
a heap of leaves till the next day. Meantime, Nausicaa,
daughter of Alcinous, king of the Phaeacians, was due
to attend to the family wash. She awoke at dawn and
in a high, strong-wheeled wagon drawn by mules,
attended by her maidens, proceeded to the river,
where she attended to the washing of the clothes and
spread them out to dry. After that she and her maidens
played ball, and the princess threw the ball into the
river. The outcry of these young things awoke Odysseus, and he came out clad only in a bush. I was de-
lighted. I had grown up near the Ohio River and knew
about rafts and storms and piles of leaves. I knew about
people in those old days who washed their clothes in
the river. I knew exactly how Odysseus felt in his trying situation and shared his modesty. I knew good
housekeeping, was charmed by the graceful but inept
way in which girls play ball, and was not indifferent
to what Homer said about how pretty the maidens
were.

    To attribute my youthful pleasure in that passage
solely to a mystical thing called art seems to me to be
nothing short of silly. The dictionary says that art is
skill, and, if it is, it is an eternal idea and a continuum.
In this case it is, as always, a concomitant. I shall even
go a little further and say that I believe with Chaucer
in *The Physician's Tale*[3] that Nature strives constantly
for perfection, and I believe it on soundly evolutionary
grounds:

> This mayde of age twelve yeer was and tweye
> In which that Nature hadde swich delit,
> For right as she kan peynte a lilie whit,

> And reed a rose, right with swich peynture
> She peynted hath this noble creature.

And I shall add Shakespeare when he has Othello say of Desdemona: [4]

> Thou cunning'st pattern of excelling nature.

There are things going on in this world undreamed of in the philosophy of theory-ridden critics. Some of those things I spoke of as eternal ideas.

The dictionary gives as a primary meaning of criticism: the action of passing judgement upon the qualities of anything. Frankly, that seems to describe an end-product of cognition—in recollection, recognition, decision or what not. I am no enemy of faculty psychology, which was deduced by great men from human behaviour, but the truth of it is that the makers of faculty psychology did not know that the mind itself was acting as a whole and that its operations are unified. It seemed well to them to introduce a special agent—in this case a faculty called judgement. In fact they procured a whole household of servants to take charge of mental processes—imagination, memory, judgement and a major-domo called Intuition. The mind itself had little to do except keep house for the Soul. It is a fiction and a very pretty one. Spenser did a beautiful job in *The Faerie Queene*.[5] Alma takes Sir Guyon to the turret of her house (the cranium) where they view the three chambers in which the principal faculties of the mind are operative. In the front chamber, greatly decorated, is Phantastes, whose function is imagination, and an idea of his operation can be gathered from the room in which he dwells, with his 'sharpe staring eyes, that mad or foolish seemed':

> His chamber was dispainted all within,
> With sundry colours, in the which were writ
> Infinite shapes of things dispersed thin;

5

> Some such as in the world were never yet,
> Ne can devized be of mortall wit;
> Some daily seene, and knowen by their names,
> Such as in idle fantasies doe flit:
> Apes, lions, AEgles, Owles, fooles, lovers, chil-
> dren, Dames.

They next visit the second chamber, that of Judgement or Reason. Its walls are decorated with the 'memorable gestes' of wizards, magistrates, counts, tribunals, commonwealths, states, policy, laws, judgements and decretals:

> All arts, all science, all Philosophy,
> Of those that roome was full, and them among
> There sate a man of ripe and perfect age,
> Who did them meditate all his life long,
> That through continuall practise and vsage,
> He now was growne right wise, and wondrous-
> sage.

The third chamber at the back of the head, 'seemed ruinous and old'.

> And therein sate an old man, halfe blind,
> And all decrepit in his feeble corse,
> Yet lively vigour rested in his mind,
> And recompenst him with a better scorse.
> Weake body well is chang'd for minds redoubled
> forse.

But the old man is not alone, as this strophe shows:

> Amidst them all he in a chaire was set,
> Tossing and turning them withouren end;
> But for he was vnhable them to fet,
> A little boy did on him still attend,
> To reach, when euer he for ought did send;
> And oft when things were lost, or laid amis,
> That boy them sought, and vnto him did lend;
> Therefore he Aramnestis cleped is,
> And that old man Eumnestes, by their propertis.

It is very pretty, but what we have instead of this is some nine billion neurons connected by innumerable synapses, and there seems to be no need for Phantastes, Judgement and Eumnestes to supervise thinking. We know almost nothing about its processes. We merely know that it is automatic. Faculty psychology is a fiction that must not be suffered to get in the way of a unified action of the mind.

Therefore there seems no reason to permit criticism or judgement to usurp the throne, for, after all, judgement is merely an end-product of cognition and not the only one.

There is another matter that needs to be further considered. I believe that the relativistic theory of cognition is plausible and that it applies to discursive fields of learning and thought as well as to physics and the natural sciences. Art is defined as skill, sometimes as skill directed by intelligent purpose. If so, it is clearly a continuum ranging from the simplest operations of childhood and savagery to the finest of fine arts. I remember that when I was a child I decided to construct a cart. I had two empty spools, a short stick, a match-box and a string, and I made the cart in spite of the withering ridicule of my brothers and sisters. A great scholar whom I knew explained his natural bent towards art as inherited from his father, who was head horseshoer at a great racecourse. I have seen great artists in the piecing of quilts and I am opposed to having this continuum of skill and design cut through vertically in such a way as to exclude any of the free constructive activities of men and women from consideration, and refuse to believe that there is an exalted and inexplicable superhuman thing to be separated and called art. I believe the delusion is a step-child of faculty psychology.

But I should perhaps go a little further still, since the matter has been extensively debated and discussed. My object is only to make my conception of the impact of the new epistemology on literature as a free art clear. I. A. Richards in *Principles of Literary Criticism*,[6] Chapter II, 'The Phantom Aesthetic State', says, after discussing Kant's legacy of the True, the Good and the Beautiful and the tradition it established,

It requires some audacity to run counter to such a tradition, and I do not do so without reflection. . . .
The case for a distinct aesthetic species of experience can take two forms. It can be held that there is some unique kind of mental element which enters into aesthetic experiences and into no others. . . .
Alternately, the aesthetic experience may contain no unique constitutent, and be of the usual stuff but with a special form. . . .

He rejects both, on the ground that aesthetic emotion as emotion is not discriminable from other feelings arising from sentiments, and adds:

This view of the arts as providing a private heaven for aesthetics is . . . a great impediment to the investigation of their value. The effects upon the general attitudes of those who accept it uncritically are also often regrettable; while the effects upon literature and the arts have been noticeable in a narrowing and restriction of the interests active, in preciousness, artificiality and spurious aloofness.

It may be mere commonplace, but it is striking the way in which *Iliad* exemplifies McDougall's list of sentiments derived from instincts, innate tendencies and emotions of the most simple and most elemental kinds. Jealousy and resentment underlie the quarrel between Achilles and Agamemnon. Combats, such as that between Menelaos and Paris and between Ajax and Hector, with the terrible battle over the body of

Patroklos are matters of both self-defence and aggression and with them the element of competition. Shame is behind the treachery of Pandaros and blackens Achilles for ever for his mistreatment of the dead body of Hector. The valour of Diomedes feeds the tendency towards display, Curiosity attends the spectacle of Patroklos in the armour of Achilles, and both curiosity and wonder appear in the new armour of Achilles wrought for him by Hephaistos. Gregariousness is illustrated in the lists of assembled warriors, and the savage instinct for contrivance comes out in the cleverness of Odysseus and Diomedes as spies. The parental instinct and the emotion of tenderness are recorded once for all in the parting of Hector from Andromache and Astyanax, and in the last book almost nothing can equal the dignified self-abasement of Priam and the bitter grief of Andromache. A sort of warrant for the belief that literature lives on from age to age because of its organic appeal to human nature and human fate is perhaps in some measure justified by the history of *Iliad*. It was the text-book of the Greeks in their great age and has appealed to humanity always, perhaps even in the twentieth century.

It is interesting to carry this a little further, and the means of doing so is to be found in Plato. To him thought was an affair of abstraction and abstractions. He was the greatest of metaphysicians and in his skill as a thinker proceeded with a certainty that has possibly never been equalled. The most advanced of the philosophers of our time, largely through the development of symbolic logic, have attempted to render the processes of abstraction and classification more intelligible and practical, so that hope is entertained for definiteness and concinnity on higher levels of thought. As everybody knows, Plato taught the actuality of ideas and regarded them as the guarantee of definite knowledge. He used a method suited to the investigation of discursive subjects, namely, the testing of experience or Socratic inquisition. It is still available to scholars. He sought to define and establish eternal ideas, such as that of the Good and the Final Cause.

What had happened was this. Greek culture had advanced to a point where the desire for knowledge was no longer content with the sentiments, tendencies and emotions arising from event, and mentality itself was under examination. *Iliad*, along with much else, therefore became the raw material in the search for stable and predictable values. Cities and populations had come into existence, and the conduct of the individual and of society had become matters of importance. *Gorgias*, for example, begins with a discussion of the social function of rhetoric or oratory, and this leads to the subject of true happiness, which turns out to be one and the same with virtue. Behind the dialogue lies the justification of a life of philosophy or teaching as opposed to political life, and this issue has been thought to be personal to Plato. *Theaetetus*, after considering three possible definitions of the nature of knowledge and rejecting them, leaves the problem unsolved but makes progress and seems connected with *The Sophist* in the idea that Not-Being has a relative existence and that Being is a universal, and so on in other familiar dialogues. *The Republic* is after all possibly the greatest work on education ever written, and education is possibly the most difficult and most important enterprise that confronts society. An obvious case of movement towards rationalization is to be seen in Shakespeare's treatment of the Trojan war in *Troilus and Cressida*.

These illustrations with what was said about *Iliad*

may help us to understand the vastness and the un-diminished importance of appeal to human nature and human life.

Since these appeals are many and varied, we cannot afford to classify them too sharply. What we have in the field of tragedy, for example, is a series of generaliz-ations about the nature of that dramatic form: Aris-totle and his commentators, writers on Christian tragedy (the so-called tragedy of character), and Scho-penhauer on stoical tragedy. All procedure has been based on the belief that tragedy is one definite thing. In view of the many kinds of universal ideas, there may be possible sorts of human disaster, but, as every-one agrees, there is no field in which discrimination is more difficult than in that of the emotions. Posi-tivism simply will not work, and the classifications of feelings by older psychologists are discarded as futile.

The scientific treatment of literature resulted not so much in error as in the narrowing and partitioning of the field, so much so that those aspects of the subject that may be considered as the very *raison d'être* of literature were neglected and are still actually avoided. Experience is the only process of understanding in a discursive field such as ours. I refer to enjoyment, the pursuit of wisdom, the comprehensive view and the attitude of participation. Excessive division under the scientific approach became the vogue, although the formation of classes in our area is at best a relative matter. Of the greatest practical importance was the establishment of a formal, positivistic, dogmatic atti-tude in a subject in which such a thing is particularly harmful. The facts, however, are undeniable.

A book, *Writers and Critics*[7] (Ithaca, 1944), by Pro-fessor Henri Peyre, makes it clear that in the history of literature practically all great books, books that have opened new fields and expressed new ideas, have been attacked and rejected by critics. Sometimes no doubt they have been overlooked or ignored, but, whenever they have come to the notice of the critics of their times, they have been attacked with greater or less virulence. This astonishing thesis, although soundly proved by many examples in many ages and countries, remains a mystery. The book devotes itself to the tiresome subject of the function of literature, becomes, indeed, an apology for critics and criticism. There seems, however, to be no mystery about it. Critics have habitually adopted the formal, scientific ideas of their time and have applied these with relentless positivism. There is no reason to think that critical hostility to new truth has not always been active and vicious, ready to fly out of its kennel and bite every stranger that appears, but it was not until the seventeenth century that its effects began to appear in significant form. That century was provided with positivistic theory and a positivistic attitude. It defined literature in all its forms, laid down rules governing how all literature in every formal manifestation should be prepared, what forms it should assume and what ideas it should express. After criticism formed its alliance with the book-trade, much dominant criticism became as positivistic as a cook-book. Excommunication is a familiar weapon, and its only potent enemy, which is actual experience, is slow and haphazard in its operation. Books with new and true ideas, we hope are usually saved by the judgement of ordinary human beings who know how to read.

Another example of improper separation is to be seen in a division between the production of literature and the study of literature. Many humanistically disposed persons have seen or felt the inconsistency of a culture that refuses to participate in the activities of its own subject, and they are right in their judgement. The total field again is a continuum. Scholarship has no right to refuse participation in the totality of its field or to ignore the demands of literary interpretation. There is no definitive line between knowledge and participation. Genuine culture should express itself fully and freely. There will be degrees and differences, of course, but to divide the field is to hamper those who cultivate mainly one part. Those who write need knowledge and are crippled for lack of it, and those who investigate need skill, understanding and a creative urge. There is little consolation in an unnecessary quarrel.

Classes in a discursive field are not like Aristotle's division of objects into genera and species, which have at hand confirmation by simple examination of criteria, but, if the level and method of abstraction are properly adjusted, it is perfectly possible, indeed, often has a definite particularity completely satisfactory. One has, to be sure, to exercise greater care than that demanded by material objects. For example, Aristotle, in his study of dramatic form in the *Poetics*, achieved a definition of tragedy that has been accepted as applying to all tragedy, whereas he did not define and delimit tragedy in general, but presented his findings about Greek tragedy. He classified a definite body of examples of a prevailing form.

In the English Renaissance the positivistic acceptance of literary forms was centuries old and had behind it a long history of obstruction and avoidance, but was fortunately disregarded in practice until the introduction of science into literature fixed these shackles on poets and dramatists as well as on critics. Schools and coteries make their own metaphysics and thus avoid what is, what has been and what may be, namely, the concrete present. As Whitehead puts it,[8] 'It is a world also including the activity of the past [as well as the content of the present] and the limited potentiality of the future, together with the complete world of abstract potentiality, the realm of eternal objects [universals?] which transcends, and finds ex- emplification in and comparison with, the actual course of realization.' Contexts of abstraction in fields of such breadth as ours are relativistic and difficult to construct, and the defect is not in the lack of learning and careful thought, but usually in immature generali- zation, the neglect of the total view, the acceptance of mere conjecture and the driving through and estab- lishment of hypotheses that are too narrow. When these things become the practice of whole professions they result in a general avoidance of experience in favour of an unwarranted positivism.

With the acceptance of the scientific method there appeared a slightly different kind of formalism all the more vicious because it was or was supposed to be scientific instead of merely authoritative. The subject was, as said above, sliced into periods and particular- ized forms were multiplied and specialization in the parts of parts began and has continued to this day, and our subject took on a different kind of interest, lost much of its natural appeal and became a prey of neo-classical dogmatism, and later the victim of narrow or restrictive specialization. These misfortunes, as well as the commercialization of literature, seem to accom- pany academic culture. The effects of wrong concep- tions of the process of cognition and ignorance of the capabilities of the human brain abridge the possibili- ties of human life. These things all tend to remove literature from common life and to discourage creativity. As they are, however, they are not in practice worse than what might be called the *a priori* habit, namely, procedure in accordance with theories that have no support in fact; indeed, having often no plausibility. This pseudo-science produces the completest positivism, and the voice of positivism is dogma. Dogma stops progress and discourages observation and experience, for, if matters are settled once for all, why should any mind disturb itself? The resulting state is stagnation. One might, indeed may, hope that, in the presence of a new logic, a new concept of cognition and a new epistemology, the positivistic course we have so long pursued is coming to an end and that there now appears a new direction. As said above, Einstein himself asserts the Baconian doctrine of the unity of all knowledge and goes further in its proof than any man has ever gone. If all knowledge is one, we must be included in the philosophy of relativism that explains the concept. If so, the consequences for us and for others who are in a similar situation may be far greater than we can now anticipate. One can consider it only from the perspective of one's own area, but there is no reason to think that the same situation may not exist in the study of all discursive subjects—religion, philosophy and the social sciences, as well as in the humanities.

The philosophy of relativity explains change and adjustment to change and is therefore to be regarded as a desirable or beneficial state of affairs. Change is not on friendly terms with convention and the static situation, and in the healthy life it is to be welcomed. Benefits arise from the temporary nature of things. Observation and awareness reside there. This philosophy calls forth the process of thought and discovery. Its reliance is on truth and it has no antipathy to the established and accepted if these things are in line with truth. We say this in tangled terms. Those who turn away from the flux and flow of circumstance and seek protection from the vicissitudes of life and those who merely endure hardships are both dodging a destiny that may be an opportunity. This new philosophy might create the intelligence and the courage to face facts and take action in the line of wisdom. In the present situation this suggests the possibility of renascence, and we shall return to that later.

We have been following for a very long time a materialistic course to the neglect of the human purpose of language and literature. Possibly, in spite of the performance of much excellent work in the field of fact, it is natural to hope that scholarship will expand its interest and, without neglect of factual values, will pay attention to thought on higher levels of significance. The new philosophy tells us that there are vast and as yet unknown regions to be explored. This does not mean that humanistic scholarship always or even generally neglects the interpretative aspect of its task, although it does suggest that philosophically it often has a limited scientific point of view that ties its hands. It is also suggested that the new philosophy puts a greater stress than ever on fact and merely insists that fact is ascertainable in fields whose phenomena, although actual, are not tangible.

The physical sciences, largely perhaps without knowing it, have revealed the great truth that all learning is one, and, if we have the knowledge and zeal to follow their lead, it is not beyond a sensible hope that we might at least start a great and lasting movement for the betterment of life and art. Renascence itself is an eternal idea.

CHAPTER IV

PARTIAL TRUTH

> A 'class' may be described, then, as a collection of all
> those and only those terms to which a certain *concept*
> applies. If we collect all the individuals to which the
> concept 'being a fox' applies, we form the class of
> foxes. If we would form the class of prime numbers,
> we must indicate all the items to which the concept
> 'prime number' applies. We may say, then, that a class
> is the *field of applicability* of a concept; in traditional
> logic, this field is called the extension of the con-
> cept.—Mrs. Langer, *An Introduction to Symbolic
> Logic.*

POSITIVISM IS of course as old as the hills, operated practically and pragmatically in daily life,
much older than Auguste Comte. It was dominant in mediaeval philosophy and was the nurse and
teacher of the scientific method. It has its own place
and status, but it is not the whole of philosophy. It
has been attacked and in fact displaced in the field of
physics by Einstein in his philosophy of relativity. His
theory is extremely difficult, and even a modest suggestion that this later philosophy may have application
to other areas besides physics may seem in this age of
specialization to be an impertinence. It can be shown
clearly enough that the field of the humanities and
other fields in which the possibility of experiment is
imperfect or nil suffer frustration when treated positivistically, and it may be that there are clear indications that, since discursive phenomena often assume

the status of continua and actually that judgements of fact or value in these fields are at best tentative and dependent, our field is greatly, perhaps especially, relativistic in its nature. There can be no question that positivism sometimes operates as a millstone around our necks. Freely admitting the impropriety of such utterances as these by any but the greatest specialists, one can only say that there should be no narrow specialists in such a field and that, since the matter is important, ill-trained and inadequate humanists ought to be pardoned for doing the best they can.

Let us consider obstruction in terms of examples. The range of recorded and accepted error in the study of English literature and language, perhaps of all literature and language, is great, but it is not altogether or even mainly error. It is largely incompleteness. The later nineteenth century produced many great scholars in the field of English. My favourites are ten Brink and Zupitza, but there were many more. I studied under J. M. Manly and A. S. Napier, both great scholars who were late members of the group. Manly, it should be said, was a pupil of G. L. Kittridge. Napier was a pupil of Zupitza, and Bliss Perry, under whom also I studied, convinced me of the soundness of ten Brink. These scholars were not over-specialized. They were interpreters as well as merely scholars and knew and made plain the significance of their findings. They were, relatively speaking, tolerant. They have had successors in the possession of these qualities and have them now, but not always in high places, for the habit of positivistic adherence to theories, sometimes without factual support, has grown with the growth of the scientific method and has had added to it dogma and authority quite out of keeping with our times. An attempt to add anything new is dangerous, and to dis-

agree with the tenets of established schools is thought
of as heresy.

The fact that the findings of the earlier group of
scholars were necessarily incomplete means that their
successors ought to have continued to develop subjects
and points of view as they then were. This is in accordance with the principle that all determinations of
both factual and theoretical elements should be regarded merely as working bases. Intense specialization
had begun, scholars were no longer trained in Greek
and Latin, other languages, philosophy and science.
They had, besides, a positivistic attitude that made
them think that philosophy and interpretation as such
were finished and complete. The next generation of
scholars therefore pursued courses appropriate to what
seemed to be the situation. Many of them got together
what was known, made such additions to it as they
could and issued it in better form.[1] Others deserted
scholarship and opened new lines, a thing that was
proper enough if the workers had known what had
already been investigated and had known, besides, the
metaphysics of their operation. Mainly, scholars
worked positivistically in accordance with the current
scientific method. Since, as Plato taught the world, it
is difficult to think logically on a level of abstraction,
scholars, especially since the First World War, followed the most uncertain feature of the scientific
method and sometimes proceeded *a priori* and dog-
matically. As said before, such procedure in discursive
fields without regard to the ontological principle is
productive of stagnation, narrowness and avoidance.

For example, older scholars, when they saw that the
Old English poems of the Junian MS (*Genesis, Exodus,
Daniel* and *Christ and Satan*) were based on the Holy
Scriptures, which in a secondary sense they were, they

took it for granted that these poems were original works of individual authors who had made a free selection from the Vulgate and operated as modern authors do. That is, they decided that it would be useful and satisfying to write poems on these interesting and important subjects. This innocent sounding hypothesis happens to misrepresent the exact truth and introduces a profound misunderstanding of the Middle Ages.

These original authors, one of whom was possibly Caedmon, did their work from a religious, indeed an ecclesiastical motive, and they did not go to the Vulgate Scriptures and make a free selection of materials. The services of the liturgical year, as distinguished from the Mass, were gradually assembled during the first five centuries of the Christian era. They served the purpose of commemoration and instruction and contained at various seasons throughout the year all those portions of the Bible that dealt with man's creation, fall and redemption. These readings were later included in a separate service book called the lectionary. The lections or pericopes were sufficiently extensive to tell the whole story and were the basis of the biblical knowledge of the clergy, but they were quite definite in extent, and, although they were taken from the Bible, they were not the Bible itself. The writers of the Old English *Genesis, Exodus, Daniel* and *Christ and Satan* obey the limits of liturgy and are not making free selections from the Vulgate as a whole.

In order to perform the service of the hours with completeness a large number of service books were necessary, and about the year 1200 a great and skilful condensation of these books was made and properly called a breviary. In the making of this book a great abbreviation of the *lectiones* or pericopes was necessary. They are still in a sense adequate and they follow the requirements of the liturgical year with perfect exactitude. It would follow that the lectionaries and some other service books used in the mediaeval church before the composition of the breviary were much fuller than the breviary and that these fuller citations of Scripture were in use by clerics before 1200. They were fuller than the readings that appear in the breviary, but they were not the entire Scripture.

One might say that it amounts to the same thing as if the Vulgate had been used, and doctrinally it does, but the point is that it makes the poems of the Junian MS liturgical in origin, makes them the voice of the church and makes their attribution to single authors actuated by artistic motives disastrously anachronistic.

This illustration of the true but incomplete work of older scholars, which work was accepted as final, would be less important if it did not affect erroneously Middle English religious literature. A great part of Middle English literature is religious, and such parts of it as I have been able to examine turn out to be ecclesiastical and not individually religious. This absorption in the teachings and formularies of the church does much to explain the anonymity, always resented by modern scholars, of mediaeval literature.

Another example less patent and general than the preceding may be found in a famous minor triumph of philology. Eduard Sievers saw that lines 235–851 of the Old English *Genesis* are linguistically incompatible with the rest of the poem, and his philological acumen enabled him to see that the lines called *Genesis* B were based on an Old Saxon original. He went still further and advanced the speculation that they had been translated from a lost Old Saxon poem

6

by the author of the *Heliand*. The exactitude of
Sievers' linguistic knowledge was later confirmed by
the discovery of fragments of just such a work. *Genesis*
A as it stands, without allowing for several possible
defects, follows the parts of the book of Genesis that
were embodied in pre-breviary lectionaries, so that
Genesis B is clearly an interpolation and the reason
for its inclusion is not far to seek. The book of Genesis
gives no account of the warfare in heaven, which was
a relatively new and attractive theme. It was added to
Genesis for these reasons. The fall of Lucifer is a subject that often appears by itself and is often (as in
Cursor Mundi and Comestor) obviously an addition
to the biblical story. Whether or not *Genesis* B is part
of a poem on Genesis as a whole or is a separate treatment of the fall of Lucifer is yet to be determined.[2]
Here again the brilliant, sound, but imperfect work
of the older scholar has been accepted as final and left
without necessary further development. The matter
has interest and importance in other fields, especially
that of the mystery plays. In an original form of *Le
Mistère du Viel Testament* and in Corpus Christi
plays, whose structural feature was completeness of
story from the beginning to the day of judgement, the
scene or play of the Fall of Lucifer reveals itself by
meter and form as an added, presumably later event.
Such minor matters may seem unimportant, but, when
the history of literature is full of them, one sees their
importance. The point is that Middle English literature has been thought of as settled and, with some
notable exceptions, shelved for the use of historians of
literature. Its relations with European literature are
most imperfectly determined, and its very meaning
as the voice of a long period of human existence is
conventionalized in interpretation, presented in the

form of selections and is not often read in its own context.

Worst of all there are great stalking misconceptions passed on from teacher to pupil.[3] Let us consider a few of them. In the Middle Ages there was little idea of the possibility of any new discovery. The best that could be hoped for was to regain originally lost, divine wisdom. Bacon himself argues that, since Adam gave names to the newly created creatures in Paradise, he must have been perfect in wisdom. If Adam before the fall was perfect in knowledge, then the acme of science was at the remotest part of past time.[4] This reverses, as far as we are concerned, the whole perspective of learning. Knowledge, so far as it has been rediscovered, does not belong to the finder but to God and therefore is open to all mankind. Plagiarism therefore disappears, and individual authorship becomes unimportant, especially of course among those who presented the facts and sources of religion. It is possibly harmless, although annoying, to see even great scholars continually in quest of the names of authors in such fields. Individualism as we understand it was singularly lacking, and one sees no reason why modern scholars should seek to find their own faces in the mirror of the Middle Ages. Take the case of the liturgical play of Daniel, which occurs in two forms, both excellent and both clearly marked as of liturgical origin. One is in the *Versi et Ludi* of Hilarius, the other the *Daniel of Beauvais*.[5] Since both are alike in form and function, what significance can there be in knowing that one is attributed to an author about whom nothing is known? Both are *ordines* developed within the liturgy like other Latin religious dramas. It is as appropriate to rejoice over the skill of the Beauvais *Daniel* as over the one that happens to appear in a manuscript thought to contain works by one Hilarius. A variant of the procedure is to select a highly developed liturgical play, such as the Tegernsee *Antrichristus*,[6] and treat it as if it were the original, while simpler and possibly older forms of the same theme are treated as if they were derivative from the later more enlarged and developed form.

Scholarship ought not to stop too soon; when in the pursuit of a given subject a point of high development is reached, because an opinion may arise that that subject is complete with nothing more to be done. Therefore it is advisable not to shift the area of one's interest too soon. To do so is not only a misplaced positivism, but in a field such as language and literature it is absurd.[7] Even after the work of the great philologists of the end of the nineteenth century, phonology, morphology, etymology and comparative linguistics were still imperfect, and the process of application and of further development was left most incomplete. What needed to be done was, not to drop the subject after the completion of a great dictionary as if it were at an end, but to explore other regions and aspects of language by philologists themselves. To be sure, some of these neglected fundamentals have been studied sometimes by scholars who knew language and sometimes not. But the subject instead of developing into a great organized and consistent unity was broken into several disconnected pieces and the chance was lost. The same thing is true of literature, whose history, however, is much more checkered. Not even the nexus between language and literature has been subjected to competent analysis, perhaps because it was thought that the two were separate fields and unrelated. In any case, my point is that there is plenty left to do. Facts are facts, whether in philology, literature, history or science, but they are not all discoverable in the fields of the humanities by the application of the scientific method, with which, however, there is not the least quarrel in the world except that it does not apply to discursive subjects. Truth is in our field, and our progress and our existence depend on our adoption of a broader concept of value as well as truth and a method appropriate to our ends. Meantime, we hold on tightly to science, but should not adopt its positivism except when we are confronted by hard facts.

The field of the incompleteness of knowledge is very vast, so that we cannot hope to do more than make some aspects and features of it as clear as we can. For example, we shall have to take it for granted that our culture and our progress demand that generations one after another shall know who they are and where they came from. Great scholars, great critics and various writers who have studied the field believe that, if civilization is to escape degeneration, we must hold on to our intellectual and spiritual gains. We cannot safely ignore the Bible, certain works of the ancients, certain world classics, and, it seems indubitable, the literature of our race and country—our country in this case being the English-speaking world, which, wrong or right, we shall take for granted.

The first aspect we shall consider is what may be called continuity. I cannot dispense with the idea that the culture of civilization is to a great degree cumulative, and I think that the study of the literature of the past is a chief agent for securing continuity and advancement in our culture. Specifically this means that we actually cannot afford to forget what Chaucer and the Middle Ages have to tell us. For example, Chaucer and the Middle Ages believed in the validity of eternal ideas. These universals were well descended.

They came largely from the great Boethius, some bits from Cicerto, even a good deal of Platonism from the Church Fathers and the Gospel of St. John. They had the teachings of the Scriptures. These had not been demonstrated by controlled experiment and never can be. They rested merely on the wisdom of the ages in the most carefully refined and cogent form. Chaucer expresses, illustrates and tests these ideas over and over again.[8] Is the idea of Nobility really valid? Let us observe it. The knight in the *Wife of Bath's Tale* stands up to his word given to the Loathly Lady, and she grows young and beautiful in his eyes. *The Clerk's Tale*, a most moving story, deals, not with the mistreatment of Griselda, but with the triumph of Patience based on rectitude, and the upshot is that Walter is conquered as if he had been a victim of Alexander's campaigns in the East. The story is a mere parade ground for the invincible virtue of Patience, and, finally, who is noble in the great *Franklin's Tale*? The magician from Orleans who had removed the 'rockes from the coast of Bretaigne" says that he is:

> This philosophre answerde: 'Leeve brother,
> Everiche of yow dide gentilly til oother.
> Thou are a squier, and he is a knyght;
> But God forbede, for his blisful myght,
> But if a clerk koude doon a gentil dede
> As wel as any of yow, it is no drede!'

What would it mean to our country and the future if we, as well as the men of the Middle Ages, believed that Truth is not only a matter of affairs and expression but an eternal idea worthy of ultimate trust?

> Therefore, thou Vache, leve thyn old wrecched-
> nesse
> Unto the world; leve now to be thral;

Crye him mercy, that of his hy goodnesse
Made thee of noght, and in especial
Draw unto him, and pray in general
For thee, and eek for other, hevenlich mede;
And trouthe thee shal delivere, it is no drede.

There is no reason why modern people should not
believe in the validity and effectiveness of truth. There
is nothing speculative about it; this eternal idea rests
on the experience and judgement of humanity throughout its career. Our twentieth-century culture should
be aggregative—learn continuity and faith in eternal
ideas from the Middle Ages, enterprise and intellectual freedom from the Renaissance, mental alertness
from the seventeenth century, rationality from the
eighteenth, and behaviour from the nineteenth.

Another idea firmly rooted in the mediaeval mind
is not easily designated in our language but is the
very centre of the Anglo-Saxon race. We might sym-
bolize it, as Piers Plowman does, as the Field full of
Folk. One might call it democracy but without implication as to popular government. The word should
express not only human sympathy but a recognition
of human rights. It stands for a noble and, one must
believe, an eternal idea. It has had a hard time in our
hands, although it had a great revival and recognition
during what we call the period of the French Revolution. Burke, Tom Paine and Thomas Jefferson were
its English-speaking proponents. In its life in society
it creates enemies, because it goes against the tendency
of men to prey on one another. Therefore it grows
dim and even unimportant as compared with prosperity. Prosperity, it so happens, fosters its enemies.
Wealth is said to be the parent of aristocracy, and it
may be; but, if so, one should say grandparent or great-
grandparent. Certainly the first generations of wealth

are apt to be snobs in culture and ignorant and arrogant citizens. Perhaps, after all, it is merely the eternal idea of freedom that we are talking about. If we wish to preserve the great racial tradition, neither blurred nor forgotten, we should remember that the idea of total humanity appears nowhere more clearly and naturally than in Chaucer's Canterbury pilgrims except in *The Vision concerning Piers Plowman*.[9] Piers is on the Malvern Hills and sees between the Tower of Truth and the Dungeon of Wrong the 'fair field full of folk'. There are beggars, friars, priests, nuns, hermits, lawyers and labourers. Wares are offered for sale, abstractions talk—Lady Meed, Conscience and Reason. Conscience delivers a sermon against the Seven Deadly Sins, and Repentance moves the heart of the field full of folk. They are moved to seek God's Truth. Piers shows them the way to Truth on condition that they will help him plough his half-acre. Some of them do; others are merely able-bodied beggars; but they are all merely people, and they differ and wrangle accordingly. In a different form, essentially the same broad view is in Wyclif and in many other writers.

The doctrine at the base of this simple human manifestation is perhaps the most needed thing the Middle Ages have to teach us. This doctrine is hardly recognizable in its usual statement. It is the doctrine of continuity and it arises from the tacitly but generally accepted belief that man's life on earth is a mere preliminary or propaedeutic to eternal life. From this point of view life is so short and so uncertain that, compared to eternal life, it amounts to nothing and is plainly intended to enable men and women to fit themselves for eternity, and they knew how to do this! It was a matter of good deeds in all fields of activity.

The life of their successors concerned them, so that they in turn sought to make this earth a proper place for their children and their children's children. They invented or perfected most of the permanent social institutions of the modern world: law courts, schools, parliaments and universities, hospitals, counties and parishes, city governments and what not. Some abbeys and cathedrals were five hundred years and more in building. It takes knowledge of history and a lot of reading to see and feel the grasp of this idea of continuity. Solid experience is needed in the reading of mediaeval records of public and private affairs. In our country at least there is great need of some unifying force of continuity. Without it we become a prey to wasteful and continual change. Frivolity becomes an escape from life, and, in spite of it, life becomes a bore, and that in turn requires more uninteresting frivolity and more wasteful change. One at first surprising result of this day-to-day existence is sameness and monotony—cities all alike, schools and universities all alike, men of business indistinguishable in dress and gait, and thought and speech.[10]

I do not say that a little reading of mediaeval English literature will restore these lost virtues, but I do say that their loss is serious and that knowledge would do no harm. I say also that English scholarship has stopped too soon, or rather, that reading is a continual operation and that in our haste we have left behind some most important things yet to be done. What we might learn from the Elizabethans may be inferred from *The Enchanted Glass* and from other possibly better books and particularly from earnest and careful continuation of the study of the literature of the English Renaissance. After all, the first book of *Utopia* by Sir Thomas More reveals the economic folly of the

American programme for the relief of agriculture, and Roger Ascham is more intelligent about the education of the young than we are. There is still a lot to be done in old fields.

Critics habitually judge Elizabethan dramatic authors by supposedly absolute standards, and, when an authoritative critic has pronounced judgement on an author, later critics and later historians of literature repeat his verdict like clock chimes before the striking of noon. The Elizabethan drama as a whole has, for example, been worked over and classified according to an inappropriate formal system, one that is only partially related to the plays themselves. It has been enough to say that such and such dramas were Senecan. There were translations and imitations of Seneca, but the drama, as a whole, has no fixed pattern. To the Elizabethans tragedy was still a story that turned out badly and usually ended in death, and a comedy was a story that turned out well. This is aside from minor conventions of comicality. The imposition of extraneous forms on a body of literature written from a different set of concepts, no doubt useful for purposes of comparison, has diverted the world from what the Elizabethan dramatists were trying to say about life as they saw it and from the effective skill of individual dramatic authors. This causes error and darkens the field, a vast field still in confusion.

Cambises,[11] for example, is advertised as the world's worst example of dramatic bombast. It is not so at all. Bombast arises out of self-conceit and pretended mastery. *Cambises* is the work of a beginner who was trying hard to realize an ideal of pity and fear that he did not understand. The author is no fool. He was ill-informed and to some degree unskilful. Had the students of Elizabethan drama been normally obser-

vant and less hasty in the application of positivistic
standards, they would have understood *Cambises* and
looked on it justly and with some interest. It seems
to have been written at some stage in the early years
of Queen Elizabeth's reign, when education and
learned authors were at a very low ebb indeed. Henry
VIII, in his attack on the monasteries, had wrecked
the school system, which had been only imperfectly
restored under Edward VI. The learned world and
perhaps especially the universities had been greatly
disturbed in the reign of Queen Mary. The result was
that the cultural level was very low in the earliest
years of Queen Elizabeth's reign, although the magnificently successful effort to restore learning and
creativity was beginning again.

One may say that it was a time of aspiration without much enlightenment—just the time for such a
drama as *Cambises*. It is not realized that *Gorboduc*
was a magnificent achievement, almost on a continental level, and why not? Thomas Norton and
Thomas Sackville were preferred persons in both
ability and education, able to produce before the
Queen something on the finest socio-literary level.
They did not know too much, but they did know
something about Senecan tragedy. Sidney admired
Gorboduc, but saw its faults. The time between 1558
and 1566 was a period of the crude and slow beginnings of renascence. Thomas Preston, who is plainly
printed as the author of *Cambises* in the edition of
1569, was born in 1537 and was just the right age to
have suffered from the troubled conditions of schools
and universities. Critics seem unaware of such influential conditions not only in that age but all the way
through to the death of Francis Bacon in 1626. They
treat them all as if they were or ought to have been

the products of Christ Church in Oxford or Trinity College in Cambridge in the very best periods of those noted institutions. They actually do not know that the spade-work of the English Renaissance was done in the period between 1558 and 1580 during the sincere, moral, studious and aspiring earlier years of the Queen's reign, but seem to think that somebody turned on an electric switch about the year 1590, whereas the real renascence was over by that year—except the gathering of the harvest. A Thomas Preston turned out to be an able and important man, and some of the historians of drama think, in view of that fact, that he could not have written such a bad play as *Cambises*. Do they not know that education is not confined to youthful years? The question is open of course, but the idea seems a poor one.

My impression is that Thomas Preston, or a Thomas Preston, did the very best he could in *Cambises* and that he was no fool. He seems to have written the play about 1560. He knew the moral interlude and made use of its varied, heterogeneous principles and practices. He, like his successors in drama, had no dramatic techniques, but, like Shakespeare, simply told a story on the stage by means of actors and dialogue. He narrates in dignified prose a series of tyrannical murders. He is so unskilful that it is not always clear whether the motive is fear of dethronement or a towering egotism that kills because of opposition. Perhaps Preston himself was puzzled, and nobody had noted the fact that Preston suggests formlessness. In the incredibly cruel murder of the Queen, the author wakes up a bit and actually expresses sympathy, shock and indignation. Allegorical figures—Shame, Counsel, Attendance, Diligence, Preparation, Small Ability,

Commons Cry and Commons Complaint, Trial, Proof, Execution, Cruelty, Murder appear. The author probably thought such figures were essential to drama. The list is not without ingenuity but it is, for the most part, dramatically useless. The comedy is routine stuff from interludes on a low level of low comedy. But Ambidexter, the Vice, is something else. He is a mixed character—a clown, a coward, a mischief-maker and one who rejoices in murder and sin. It is hard to tell what Preston meant, and there may be the beginnings of deeper thought in Ambidexter. All one can suggest is that there is needed a study unbiased by dramatic theory of what the Vice actually did in sixteenth-century plays.

I choose this single and obscure example in the hope that it may suggest the vast need of informed and sensible particularity leading to factually based concepts, so that we may realize and use what the Elizabethan dramatists had to say about life. To set them off in a separate compartment is indolent, stupid and stultifying.

This pointing out of our disregard of eternal ideas and other values that have been determined by thinkers and observers in past ages, could go on indefinitely from Homer to Thorstein Veblen. The one considered here is incompleteness. Few thoughtful people would deny that scholars have a broader duty than the fixing of dates, the identification of authors, the determination of texts and other purely factual matters. That might have been the end and object of science, but I do not think it ever has been, and certainly it is poles asunder from the greater scientists of the modern world. Such a narrow view, such a resting content with partial truth can never have been the whole duty of humanistic scholars. I think even that it did not fix itself on scholarship until the late nineteenth century, when it adopted more completely the methods and objects of science.

There is, however, one area of observation, thought and expression too obvious, too near at hand, too important to be omitted. It is the eighteenth century. It has moral and intellectual riches that we need and are in the way of forgetting. The period was before the separation of the American people from the mother country and concerns us all. The teachings of Bacon and other liberal and all-inclusive thinkers were still at hand and the stranglehold of science had not yet become effective. Thinkers and observers could still enter soberly into the field of discursive subjects and had not yet become convinced that no actual truth resided in those fields. The eighteenth century perceived and expressed two great eternal ideas with at least partial success. These two are Order and Freedom, and we are led perforce into politics and economics. I shall have as little to do with these 'sciences' as possible, but I was a pupil of Woodrow Wilson's and am a taxpayer, and I hate to see my taxes wasted on empirical and impractical schemes and extravagances just as if nothing at all were known about these social subjects. The idea is that these eighteenth-century thinkers were not equipped with the scientific method, which the modern social scientist has at his finger-tips. Therefore these earlier thinkers could not, it is thought, discover verifiable truth. The fallacy is revealed by the fact that this exalted method does not and cannot apply fully to these discursive subjects. The men of the eighteenth century had only their brains to rely on, and that is all their modern successors have. The latter think otherwise and have had bred in them a belief that every problem is to be solved by a discovery, although the most conspicuous recent discovery turns out to be a concealed and utterly indefensible capital levy on the people as a whole. Our ancestors were not seeking such a device as this and, if they had known about it, they were too moral and too patriotic to use it for the benefit of the rich and the robbery of the poor. But, in general, I confess that I am not a specialist and that my interest is in eternal verities.

There is no problem of comprehension in the eighteenth century, since the writers of that age took pains to make themselves entirely clear. There is first the problem of order.

The habit of quoting Pope is slipping badly, but that is not Pope's fault. He talks about us all the time in clear and accurate terms. He has 'Of the Use of Riches', and he tells Dr. Arbuthnot what commonplace bores are like and does not approve of the quest for notoriety. He gives a lot of very pertinent advice in 'An Essay on Man'. The 'Essay on Criticism' sounds like an indictment very hard to refute.

> Of all the causes which conspire to blind
> Man's erring judgment, and misguide the mind,
> What the weak head with strongest bias rules
> Is pride, the never-failing vice of fools.

By 'pride' he evidently means self-conceit. He goes on:

> Whatever Nature has in worth denied,
> She gives in large recruits of needful pride;
> For as in bodies, thus in souls, we find
> What wants in blood and spirits, swelled with wind;
> Pride, where wit fails, steps in to our defence,
> And fills up all the mighty void of sense.
> If once tight reason drives that cloud away,
> Truth breaks upon us with resistless day.
> Trust not yourself; but your defects to know,
> Make use of every friend and every foe.[12]

Addison too wants a correct, honest and orderly world and makes it very clear:

Upon the path of my father I was resolved to travel into foreign countries, and therefore left the university, with the character of an odd unaccountable fellow that had a great deal of learning, if I would but show it. An insatiable thirst after knowledge carried me into all the countries of Europe, in which there was anything new or strange to be seen, nay, to such a degree was my curiosity raised, that having read the controversies of some great men concerning the antiquities of Egypt, I made a voyage to Grand Cairo on purpose to take the measure of a pyramid; and as soon as I had set myself right in that particular, returned to my native country with great satisfaction.[13]

These two great but rather gentle advocates of law and order were companioned in those times by Jonathan Swift and other notable men who held the same general opinion, that order is the principle of civilization. Swift, except in the matter of literary style, was disorderly in behalf of order—one of the greatest satirists who ever lived. A satirist is one who employs in writing or speaking 'sarcasm, irony, ridicule, etc., in denouncing, exposing, or deriding vice, folly, abuses, or evils of any kind'. This is from the dictionary and, if we add disorder to the list of aims, we shall have Swift. I do not mean to apply any epithets to Swift, not even *trenchant*. I know him too well. But I will say that we in our age need his clear head, his moral courage and his faith in rectitude and all the eternal ideas associated with it. Not John Milton himself was more staunch.

But, as exponent of what the early eighteenth century knew and believed and was, my faith is in Anthony Ashley Cooper, Third Earl of Shaftesbury. One of the most learned and accomplished men of his time and a man who thought and wrote on a high level of abstraction, he is nevertheless devoid of obscurity and confusion—ready at all times to descend to the particular. It is difficult to choose illustrative passages from an author of such breadth, but one may lay out a small display: There is the brief life of Shaftesbury by his son, the remarkable *Philosophical Regimen*, with its thirty-four essays on basal ideas in the philosophy of life; also *Characteristics of Men, Manners, Opinions, Times*, and Shaftesbury's letters to John Locke, who was his tutor, and to many other men of importance. There is nothing crabbed or obscure about Shaftesbury's style; for example, this is the opening of 'An Enquiry concerning Virtue or Merit' from *Characteristics*:

The nature of virtue consists (as has been explained) in a certain just disposition or proportionable affection of a rational creature towards the moral objects of right and wrong. Nothing can possibly, in such a creature, exclude a principle of virtue, or render it ineffectual, except what

1. Either takes away the natural and just sense of right and wrong;
2. Or creates a wrong sense of it;
3. Or causes the right sense to be opposed by contrary affections.[14]

Thus begins a sensible and practical moral treatise.

Shaftesbury was the grandson of the First Earl of Shaftesbury, politician and probably statesman in the troublous times of the Rebellion, the Commonwealth and the reign of Charles II, his reputation with posterity much blackened by Dryden's brilliant satire *Absolem and Achitophel*, in which he appears as the unscrupulous Achitophel. In the eyes of his grandson he appeared as a man who disliked autocratic power in government. Our Shaftesbury was right in this, and he himself, although he does not write extensively on

7

political matters, was a firm but reasonable liberal and therefore forms a bridge of political liberalism from an earlier time to that of the reign of George III.

The liberals of that age are close at hand in both Great Britain and the United States, for both countries in their different ways have established governments of the people. In my youth the doctrine of individual freedom was well known and much studied in schools and colleges and was done from a quite definite point of view. Liberty was thought of as a slowly achieved ideal of Anglo-Saxon civilization, and Burke was the main authority. There was of course the speech *On Conciliation with the Colonies*, but that *On American Taxation* and even the *Letter to the Sheriffs of Bristol* were by no means unknown. The point is that we read the *Reflections on the Revolution in France* and agreed with Burke cordially. We knew a little about Rousseau and Tom Paine, but did not approve of them because they seemed to be actuated by theoretical considerations, whereas we preferred to think that civil librty under the law was an achievement of our race. I know how offensive to certain fanatics is the idea that Americans belong to the same race as the British, but such seemed to be the facts. We liked Jefferson and knew a little about him, in part perhaps because he agreed with Burke. Later in my own case I had the, let us say, organic concept of liberty reinforced in me when I studied under Woodrow Wilson, then professor of history and politics at Princeton. Indeed, that is the last special work I ever did on the subject. Wilson was in strong agreement with Burke in the doctrine of liberty under the law and amplified Burke's idea with Jefferson and Bagehot, with many others and with his own penetrative insight.

What I say would be out of line were it not for the

special situation of the eternal concept of human freedom, which runs counter to a tendency of human beings to enslave their fellow human beings. This is a powerful and determined instinct or tendency that continues on every sort of captious and professed moral intention and in very subtle ways to have its will. This has caused me to suggest in this chapter that scholarship is not merely a matter of finishing subjects up, binding them with red tape or rubber bands and sticking them in pigeon-holes. I believe that scholarship has a continuing function and a duty to society in this and other matters. Perhaps I should not have discussed this if I had seen or heard the least mention of Edmund Burke since the First World War. I do not think it safe for this country to neglect him and the ideas that he stood for. I think it a vital matter. The modern way of looking into such matters does not seem to me to go after the truth in a scholarly way. I do not think it sound logic to arrive at a decision between black and white to the effect that the result is grey or that foxes should be consulted about every issue that concerns poultry.

There are many other cases in which the recorded experience of the past concerns the modern world deeply, which cannot dispense with continuity. It has been argued that truth in discursive fields is revealed solely by intelligent induction from experience and not by discovery or broad intrusion of wrongly applied scientific theories. It takes time to build a civilization, and continuity is the answer. More specifically, scholarship must not stop too soon, since it has a continuing duty to society in the determination of truth.

There are other aspects of partial truth; for example, conclusions based on inadequate data, but they will be better treated elsewhere. Here we have tried to show how much remains for scholars to do. It would, however, be an instance of stopping too soon if I should fail to quote one of the many things that Milton has to say about freedom:

For who loves that, must first be wise and good.

And add his statement in prose: 'For, indeed, none can love freedom heartily but good men; the rest love not freedom but license.' With this condition we understand the Gospel of St. John (viii. 32): 'The truth shall make you free.'

CHAPTER V

ANACHRONISM

Dah's de stump, dah—dat's one er de women; heah's
you—dat's de yuther one; I's Sollermun; en dis yer
dollar bill's de chile. Bofe you claims it. What does I
do? Does I shin aroun' mongs' de neighbors en fine
out which un you de bill *do* b'long to, en han' it over
to de right one, all safe en soun', de way dat anybody
dat had any gumption would? No; I take en whack
de bill in *two,* en give half un it to you, en de yuther
to de yuther woman. Dat's de way Sollermun was
gwyne to do wid de chile. Now I want to ast you:
what's de use er dat half a bill?—can't buy noth'n
wid it. En what use is half a chile? I would'n give a
d͜ for a million un um.—Mark Twain, *Huckle-
berry Finn.*

ANACHRONISM IS annoying to scholars, who
think they have learned by honest effort what
Chaucer, Shakespeare and Milton said and what
these great poets and other poets said and what they
meant when they said it. They find, however, the
matter taken out of their hands. When this is done by
the ordinary ill-informed world, who possibly make
most final decisions, it makes less difference. The an-
noyance comes from impostors and egotists who mis-
lead the world before one's eyes, and serious false
interpretations become current. This is the more dis-
pleasing to scholars, because they believe with good
reason that the actual meaning of the literature of the
past is what the world needs and would approve of and
enjoy. It is no small matter, they think, to have com-

89

monplace and pretentious substitutes for great poets. There is therefore a distinction to be made that carries with it an adjustment and a sort of consolation. The situation is old as well as new, and in the light of experience these greater voices have made themselves audible to all sorts and conditions of men and in all probability will continue to do so. But let there be no mistake, the literature of the past is the end and aim of humanistic study. Let the modern age speak for itself in its own voice.

There is no great principle at stake in the avoidance of anachronism, which is mainly due to an inability to understand and allow for change in an accepted order of social beliefs. A family, let us say, moves from what they believe is the centre of social propriety into a different country, one that from the point of view of this family is in its inevitable differences less refined or less generally satisfactory. There is a choice to be made. The immigrant family may adapt themselves sufficiently to the ways, even the tastes, of their new neighbours, or they may adhere with greater or less strictness to the, to them, better habits and social attitudes of their beloved home land. They may be right in their choice of this road to satisfaction, and, if they are just and upright people, they will usually escape censure, although they will probably be labelled with the name of a foreign country, since they do not understand their new surroundings. This spectacle, frequently seen in a country like the United States, is merely narrowness of culture. This hypothetical family might retain the virtues of their nativity and without conflict acquire new ones. So it is to some degree when one moves into the Middle Ages and finds before him the *Franklin's Tale* in Chaucer. The visitor might readily understand and accept the idea of Nobility. He might be able to suspend his incredulity in the matter of moving the rocks on the coast of Brittany if it were well enshrouded in hocus-pocus about appearance and reality. But he would possibly break down somewhere —perhaps when asked to believe in the malady of love, a disease so deadly as to justify the brother's resort to magic in order to save the life of Aurelius. This analogy is remote enough, but it is intended to suggest that difference or change have to be heeded.

To describe the sufferings of the Middle Ages and the Renaissance from anachronistic thinking is a gigantic undertaking and a thing that is hard to do and at the same time to maintain an objective and friendly attitude. It is no doubt natural enough for living people to think that, let us say, the writing and staging of plays in those two long periods were exactly as they are today. In a completely ignorant form, such as it was in Chaucer's and Shakespeare's times, anachronism is not offensive, has in fact a certain naïve merit and directness. It is less allowable when one realizes that the scholars of our own time often employ assumptions based on anachronistic thinking and stoutly supported by positivism. This becomes of far-reaching extent in the creation and perpetuation of error when scholars disregard, or are unbecomingly ignorant of, the philosophy or the accepted way of thinking and of acting in any past times such as the Middle Ages and the Renaissance. It is not a matter of wrong and right; it is a matter of understanding. And, besides, these bygone ages excelled us in many ways.

The stream of consciousness in the human mind is itself a continuum made up in the first instance of sensations, perceptions, urges, ideas and occupations that constitute the elements of an immediate present;[1]

but there are also in this continuum recollections of
an already completed past perhaps of a second or less,
a day, a month, a year or many years. These may be
events, emotions, ideas of good or ill, folly or wisdom
or what not that belong in their urgency to the past.
But they do not stop with the present but constitute a
third element in the continuum, namely, anticipation
of the future. Thus the present, the past and the future
combine to make up a total present.[2] Some of these
constituents are merely there in a perceptive vividness,
some are wholly in the past with varying degrees of
potency for the here and now, and others look to the
future. Error and vagueness may appear everywhere,
but it is possibly the interpretation and adjustment
of these factors that constitute practical wisdom.

It is probable that in some minds there is little that
has to do with the past or the future and that affairs
of the active present prevail. Such limited minds are
not necessarily worse than others except, let us say,
for certain purposes. Our interest as students of literature centres in this point, since our interest is in the
restoration of the dead past to a living present. We
even think that the ability to restore the past in the
field of literature depends on education and experience, also on unselfish interest, the logic of fact and
idea, and the ability to pass in our interests beyond the
self of the immediate world. Those who lack interest in
the past are liable to have no sense of the past, even the
idea that there is such a thing or that, if there is such
a thing, it does not and cannot concern them and their
affairs. If they perceive such a past thing, it is to them
merely an ictus of the here and now. We may say
moderately that such persons are not well suited for the
task of writing history or of interpreting literature,
especially the literature of other ages and countries,

where one meets with different philosophies, beliefs, customs and conditions from those that prevail in a world dominated by the living present.

We have to do with a continuum of course in which there is the disposition to interpret the past as a part of the current world. The ability to live imaginatively in the past and to enter the minds and hearts of others, even of those long dead or of those whose deeds and motives come to us in the shadowy outlines of mythology and romance, is rare. The interpretation of the literature of the past or of different ages and races in terms of the present we regard as a form of anachronism, as a varying tendency of varying degrees of dominance.

In its simple form it does not do much harm. The Elizabethan disposition to think of Cicero and Cataline as contemporary created an intimacy and was rather naïve and sweet. Indeed, factual anachronism, even when it results in obvious error, is in practice much less harmful than are anachronistic generalizations that do injury, either by praise or blame, to ages, authors and groups of authors. It has been, as we shall see, our practice to embody these anachronistic opinions in authoritative histories and to base literary education, not on the works themselves, but on concatenations of more or less anachronistic generalizations. If the literary works of the past were approached and actually mastered in an open-minded search for truth, the harm again would be negligible, especially as it would be gratifying to knock these anachronistic idols over. But they are saved by authority or by positivistic thinking. There can be no value, but actual harm, in building a literary education, on any level, out of an often pompous series of partly anachronistic generalizations. We pause long enough to say again that there is no road to understanding and wisdom in any discursive field except that of experience. This means that, even on an elementary level, it is better to have books read, understood and enjoyed than to have them merely criticized. There are those who defend the interpretation of literature in terms of what it is thought to mean here and now in disregard of the author's actual meaning. There is no statute against this, but it might be more honest to say, not 'Shakespeare said so and so', but 'I think Shakespeare ought to have said so and so'.

Our interest in anachronistic thinking is thus limited to its error-producing features in scholarship and criticism. Anachronism as a producer of wide and harmful error ranks very high, certainly on a par with strict adherence to authority, *a priori* dogmatism, and even positivism in the concepts of knowledge and truth.

Let us illustrate this from the English religious drama, which was part of a European manifestation that can be understood, although an adequate understanding depends on knowledge of mediaeval religion and mediaeval life. Religion must be known because this drama was the offspring of the Church and never deserted its creator. One must know the unity of the mediaeval church as a vast and co-ordinated system, a unity and a co-ordination, however, that was so well adapted to human life in its age that they admitted an astonishing variety in their adaptation to the conditions of a vast territory and for a long period. The mediaeval church cannot be said to have been positivistic except in a relatively small number of crucial matters. It has been thought that certain secular qualities of the religious drama are inconsistent with religious dominance. The answer to this, as we shall see, is that mediaeval men and the mediaeval church expected all but a very few selected saints to be secular. A saint was not an angel but a glorified and sanctified human being.

To quite as great a degree understanding of the religious drama depends on knowledge of the Middle Ages. Mediaeval philosophy was no haphazard system, but was definite and stable without being hostile to change provided that change was in the direction of the realization of God's kingdom on earth. Indeed, mediaeval teachings and beliefs constituted a philosophy of growth towards perfection and had, besides, an idea of continuity extending not through a human life only but through eternity. Human life was pupilage, a brief period of test and effort prefatory to life through eternity. It was not to be despised but to be used, and the result of this is a record of order and persistence unequalled perhaps in human history. The mandates of God demanded order, and the Middle Ages instituted most of the organizations with which we live—universities, courts of law, parliaments, kingship, eleemosynary institutions and many others. Its doctrine of social persistence displays itself in the building of cathedrals and churches extending sometimes for centuries, a thing that indicates institutional efficiency, on the one hand, and persistence in good works on the other. This striving for completeness and perfection appears in great patient books like *Acta Sanctorum, Summa Theologica,* and the corpus of divine services as presented in the Breviary, itself a long, detailed and consistent book which is an epitome of many books. Among mediaeval institutions is the vast and varied dramatization of the story of man's fall and redemption, a work so large that beyond a strictly liturgical early stage within the church, it covered in its ramifications the whole spiritual life of mankind. The religious drama in various vernaculars, of which perhaps nine-tenths have been lost, is too large to admit of collection; all this devoted formally to a vast concept of man's existence on earth and his preparation for life in eternity. The concept that is presented is very simple and is subsumed under two words: Fall and Redemption. This concept is completely inclusive. No man can escape the consequences of the Fall, and all men desire Redemption. It includes all men and admits every human being in every possible situation. No great concept has ever been so all-embracing.

Drama is described as a representative art in time and space and has as its criteria impersonation, dialogue and action or event. The greatness of drama both in the ancient and the modern world has convinced us that in the matter of presenting human beings and their actions drama is the master art. But in the Middle Ages, drama, even the knowledge of what it was, had disappeared, and we might say that the Middle Ages needed drama badly. They did not know what drama was, but they rediscovered the form. A trope, earliest performed at St. Gall, happened to demand impersonation, dialogue and action in its performance. Drama creates suspense, and suspence demands fulfilment. This happened and in a way very characteristic of the Middle Ages, that is, by incremental expansion, at first with tiny bits of liturgy and later by related episodes. Thus a drama of the Resurrection grew to completion in terms of the service. It was perhaps a century and a half before it was recognized as actual drama and longer than that before it strove for any popular appeal. Its limitation was in the religious service and its appeal was religious. It lacked throughout its career any liberty to select its own subjects for treatment, and, although in its last century of existence it took subjects other than those supplied by the cursus of the liturgical year, it always adhered to the liturgy, which embodied religious truth. It took its principal novelties from New Testament Apocrypha, which were as true to the age as canonical Scripture.[3]

This is a story of plain fact known to scholarship for three quarters of a century, embodied in scores of books and articles of the highest authority and yet somehow never taken into the minds of critics and historians of literature and never thought of as significant or definitive. Religious drama was great enough in size, long enough in practice, and engaged the interests of enough people to merit a better fate. It may be that to regard the religious drama as a dramatic activity that existed for itself and its own special ends conflicts with a great anachronistic and *a priori* theory. Drama has been the favourite child of criticism for a century or more. All persons with pretence to literature know what it is now, and some of them, less perfectly, what it was in the age of Shakespeare. It is said to be drama, and they think they know exactly what drama is and how it is written and produced. A modern dramatist desiring to write a religious drama would take a copy of the Authorized Version of the Bible, look it over, select a subject, make a scenario and write the play. Mediaeval playwrights, they think, must have done just these things, and, if their plays met with popular approval, the names of their authors ought to be at least in the larger biographical dictionaries. But the religious drama did not come into existence and achieve its first great growth in any such way. These plays were written bit by bit, or at least episode by episode, through hundreds of years. There were no theatres, no gate receipts, few, if any, professional actors, and the purpose was not entertainment but worship of God and instruction in His word. Books from publishers of good standing come out year by year whose authors do not know the criteria of the definition of the dramatic form, think that any manipulation of pageantry, impersonation or *mise en scène* is drama, and repeat with approval the long-discarded theory that the religious drama originated in dumbshow. The best they have to say about this great literary manifestation that lasted five hundred years and satisfied the interests of perhaps millions of people is that it was an ignorant and rather puerile exercise that served nevertheless as a preparation for the drama of the Elizabethans. Drama is no such narrow thing as that. These enthusiasts do not even know that the greatest gift of the mediaeval drama to, say, Shakespeare was that it had no technique of the drama, no definitions and no rules. That was a real gift, and one of the greatnesses of Shakespeare is that he disregarded theorists and authorities and simply told a story by means of a stage and a company of actors.

Another illustration of less importance from the same field has to do with the morality play, whose nature and origin may never be understood, although nothing could be simpler. The dictionary says an allegory is 'the description of a subject under the guise of some other subject of aptly suggested resemblance'. The moralty play is a dramatized allegory. This fact was pointed out by the late Professor J. M. Manly in his epoch-making article, which is an illustration of the construction of hypotheses on a level of literary forms.[4] Mediaeval literature is full of allegorical elements, and the presence of allegorical figures and allegories themselves in drama does not change the nature of ordinary drama devoted to the representation of characters and events. When the allegory itself was made into a play, certain convincing characteristics made their appearance. Personal reactions ceased and action took place on a plane of inevitability. In the most important respect also the morality play generalized the concept of the fate of man on earth. It advances again the basal theme of the mystery play, namely, man's proneness to sin, his fallen state, and his quest for salvation. Indeed, even in restricted aspects, there is a central idea of the fate of man in some age or status or of an institution or a cause endangered by sin and the powers of evil. A character allegorically representative of man proceeds more or less according to pattern. Born in sin and as yet innocent, he passes into youth, meets with a sin or vice which says, 'Come with me'. He does so without a struggle, lives in sin for a time and then meets Repentance in some allegorical figure and again obeys its counsel with complete objectivity and mends his own life. Man usually, however, falls from grace and meets death, also allegorical, still doomed. He is then saved by simple perseverance and the mercy of God or by some intercession. There are of course many varieties and degrees of fidelity to the basal form. But this factual account is constantly rejected by a debased form of the idea of the evolution of literature made current during the nineteenth century by Brunetière and others.

False theories, invented or inherited, distort every field they comprise in their scope, large or small. This furnishes a reason why literature should not be presented in terms of the generalizations of others but should rest squarely on experience. The outward show may be less impressive, but the comprehension of significance, the only thing that counts, will be in the end effective.

Take the case of the conception of tragedy. Here we have a nobly descended concept derived from Aristotle, presenting a partial truth capable of wide application without violation of actuality. Aristotle makes tragedy rest on the Greek concept of human existence and human fate. The idea conforms to rise and fall, ebb and flow, youth and age, and accounts so satisfactorily for most varieties of the human career that it has served well to describe the tragedy that besets humanity and continues to serve.

But it is not a generalization whose criteria are complete. Let us see if this can be made clear. The tragic course is this. Man struggles upwards to a point of triumph, but, having reached this summit, fate or destiny or the gods themselves refuse to grant the perpetuity of success, and the man is stricken down and ends in disaster. Aristotle says that such spectacles purge the emotions of the spectator through the agency of pity and fear, and surely this is the most profoundly moving aspect of existence and the most inclusive. One can only ask if other situations than success turning into failure produce pity and fear in the prospect of existence. This is at least worth enquiring into, for, if there should be other sources of such emotions, they deserve recognition. One cannot be too definite, for it is unprofitable to analyse emotions into rigid classes.

Aristotle's definition of tragedy is the greatest ever made, but it may not be the exact and final statement it has been thought to be. It is a brilliant and sound formulation of a class and thus forms a definition of Greek tragedy as Aristotle knew it. He said that tragedy is the imitation of a painful action (usually resulting in death) that by pity and fear effects a purgation of these emotions in the spectators. He makes in the *Poetics* a statement, overlooked by commentators, of great importance in this connection, namely, that drama concerns itself with event and not with character. Aristotle's definition has been narrowed by translators. The word we translate as 'pity' is ἔλεος and the one we translate as 'fear' is φόβος. Both are words of general inclusiveness and rich connotation, so that a whole group of kindred emotions is included under or suggested by these words. Aristotle says that tragedy is due to the inevitable or the unexpected; that is, to fate or accident.

Christianity could not accept the concept of life underlying this, and it invented, mainly in the Renaissance, a theory of tragedy that suited it; that is, hamartia or tragic guilt. From this came the concept of the tragedy of character according to which it has been said that character is fate. This idea of course was not and could not be absent from Greek tragedy, but it contributed another eternal idea on the highest level of abstraction. Theology tells us that the main functions of God are creation and redemption, and redemption may be said to be a universal human need. Therefore failure to achieve redemption is tragic.

There is also in the doctrines of stoicism the possibility of still another sort of true tragedy. Indeed, the two great tragedies of Seneca, *Hercules Furens* and *Hercules Oetaeus*, seem to be ancient examples of this form. It seems also to appear in essence in *Prometheus Vinctus*. According to this principle life is or may be hostile all the way through and a tragic instance appears when the ills of life are borne with a courage, patience and persistence only to be overcome by death itself. It may be that we here have to do with another eternal idea, since courage, patience and persistence are

8

part of the creative aspect of the Almighty, on which a generalization on the highest level may be made.

This context of tragic abstraction is moreover probably not yet complete. For example, *The Trojan Women* of Euripedes and other Greek tragedies seem to derive their tragedy from group suffering. It is hard to account for *Richard III* on the Aristotelian principle. The play arouses pity and fear or kindred emotions, but they are derived from the sufferings of Richard's victims. The play presents an odious event that may happen to people, and must indeed be known and experienced freely in the sufferings and oppressions of the tyrannous world as we know it. This means that tragedy is not a mere literary form but a feature of life itself. Shakespearean tragedy cannot, except with the loss of comprehension, be confined within Aristotelian limits. The same is true of Ibsen and other modern writers of tragedy. If this is true, we should study tragedy as exemplary of certain eternal ideas derived from knowledge and experience of life and not merely from literary patterns. There is no pigeonhole big enough to hold all tragedies, and to crowd them in to it is to misunderstand them and devitalize them.

Take two examples from Shakespeare. *Othello*, often described as Shakespeare's tragic masterpiece, has been over-simplified and not fully understood. Othello's tragedy is not merely his defeat by evil but also his failure to achieve salvation, for Desdemona's sweetness, gentleness, and purity almost but not quite save his soul. *Coriolanus* is regularly misunderstood. It is thought of, even by Plutarch, as the example of a man who falls a victim to the passions of pride, revenge and anger, this in accordance with the Galenic or stoical psychology. The hero's sparing of Rome is explained in actual trivial ways, although the reason is clearly stated. It is also said that Shakespeare yields to patriotism. In point of fact he yields at the expense of his life to something far deeper than patriotism, an eternal idea that is the foundation of love of country. His family are part of himself and are the basis of ultimate human survival. Little Marcius, who 'kneels and holds up hands for fellowship, is the symbol of this. Rome, corrupt, ungrateful and vicious, amounts to nothing. Coriolanus has been carried to the threshold of damnation, and 'The gods look down, and this *unnatural scene* they laugh at'. No choice could be more tragic than Coriolanus has to make. It is life we study and must know. Literary theories and conventions are mere diversions that fence us off from the actual.

We know what the literary theorists of the Enlightment did. They went back rather misunderstandingly to Aristotle through his continental followers and proceeded to make not only the forms but the subject-matter of literature into a science. Drama, lyric, epic and other sorts of poetry, with various kinds of prose, became what Pseudo-Aristotle said they were. There were subjects proper to literature and subjects unfit for literary treatment. Poetry and prose were separated by barriers as were matter and spirit. The new psychology was called on for distinctions (no longer considered valid) among the products of imagination, fancy and memory.[5] Pure literature became a mystery. Poets were no longer people; they were supermen.

Forms were regarded, and I am sorry to say still are, not as inventions and general concepts arising out of the application of logic to particular subjects and conditions but as immutable and original, as if God had said, 'Let there be comedy (preferably social and suited to the tastes of the upper classes) and tragedy (of the pseudo-Aristotelian kind) and lyric, satire and the rest', and these things were. Only stubborn geniuses like Bunyan and Fielding broke through the barriers. Acuteness of mind and refinement of analysis produced and continue to produce endless distinctions, great volumes of criticism and whole schools of literature. The structure is now so great and secure that it seems futile to declare that organized literary criticism, except when it is interpretative and true to fact, is a vast post-Cartesian fabric ill-adapted to both literature and life. Criticism has had an erroneous idea of the true nature of genius, which it has prevailingly regarded as a supernatural manifestation in literature (and of course criticism). Art is not divine; it is merely a feature of constructive action and is a continuum without break from mere chaos to the most perfect products of poetry, painting, sculpture and music. Have these theorists never seen a great woodman fell a tree with an axe? It is no wonder that in this world of affectation and fallacy men of ability have held themselves aloof, and that literature, which is the voice and record of human life, has become a specialty often despised by men of action and accomplishment.

Somewhere along the road men interested in literature and not merely in speculation about literature, men who knew that actual things have interest and importance, withdrew themselves, often humbly, into the fields of fact and narrowed the word scholar as their designation. This created a division between scholarship and criticism that still exists. Although both groups were possibly happier after the break was made than before, it is a most unfortunate separation —ignorant critics have the ear of the public, and the men who know refuse to speak. Truth is not limited to established fact. Scholarship and interpretation are not properly separable in function. They form a continuum of elements of one function and are not properly separable. It is in fact erroneous and harmful to draw a line between them. How the breach can ever be healed in this partitioned world is hard to see, and yet the solution is simple and with a change of philosophy might be possible. The possibility of a change from specialization to the broadest possible knowledge is the main subject treated in this book.

These foregoing cases of anachronism are mainly those in which authoritative judgements were made after the fact. Aristotle was made to say things he did not say, important things he did say were overlooked or disregarded, and his determinations about Greek literature in the fourth century B.C. were made to apply to all literature in all ages. This type of thinking is a natural enough tendency to interpret everything in terms of critics and their own times and not in terms of authors and their times. The history of criticism presents therefore a spectacle of anachronism broken here and there by truer insight or insight into the actual. Earlier critics, such as Boileau or Dryden, are not to be blamed for not knowing Aristotle's meaning, which was a difficult thing to understand, indeed was not fully understood until the late nineteenth century, nor could it be denied that neo-classical critics had clear and consistent meanings of their own. Who knows, moreover, whether Horace and the Italian Aristotelians knew that there were actual differences in such things as poetry and drama, for literature was a thing as definite as footwear. It is, of course, but the world is more varied than feet.

In any case, these actual errors are subject to easy correction when the truth is known; slow of course.

There are still scholars who believe that tragedy is exactly what Aristotle said it was, but they are dying off. If we use the word anachronism in its ordinary sense, to mean an error in chronology by which events are misplaced in regard to each other, especially the error of misunderstanding and misinterpreting past events in terms of the present, that is, as if they had happened, or been uttered, at this place within the last few weeks, one wonders how it comes about. It is usually said that those guilty of this error lack historical imagination, and, from the point of view of faculty psychology, they certainly do. But that statement really tells us nothing. One might as well say that such persons are ignorant and undeveloped mentally and have no concepts beyond the range of a restricted present. Perhaps, for the most part, they are ill-taught. If they have read any part of the Bible or of history, they have not understood it. One can forgive this and strive to correct it. But such a state of mind in professional critical and dramatic producers is less easy to forgive. We are not, however, satisfied with 'lack of the historical imagination' as descriptive of the situation, for it seems to remove the blame from the whole man or woman and place it on a third party known as imagination. The presumption is that, if one gave the ill-educated kind of anachronists a small package of historical imagination, he or she would be cured. This is not true; it would take many doses along with study and thought to affect a cure. To me the violence done to Shakespeare by quite respectable companies of players and by well enough known Shakespeare critics has been nothing short of desecration and sinful misrepresentation.

We need to understand the nature of the record of the past as it appears in the present, and it is not hard to understand. There are elements in human life that seem, so far as one can see, to resist the elapse of ages, the change of customs and the various stages of culture. It was suggested in a previous chapter that these unchanging things are evolutionary in their origin. I am sorry that I am not a specialist in the field of biological, and especially human, evolution, but I have read a good deal about it and had in college a very good course in descriptive zoology, and I do not think that I am wrong. The problem interests me in this connection and in general. When I quoted McDougall in a preceding chapter,[6] I did so because he seemed to provide us human beings with a common and inevitable set of emotions, sentiments, motives, and, in general, responses to existence, and I think he meant to do so. If we have such a basis of feeling and thought and if literature appeals to it, anachronism disappears, but if we add to the sum of the space-time continuum things that Shakespeare did not know or intend, if the values we apprehend are special to ourselves and unknown to Shakespeare or are things he never dreamt of, anachronism reappears. This, at any rate, seems a sort of working basis.

Now Shakespeare was a dramatist of surprisingly wide and varied appeal and marvellous clarity, so that he can be trusted. We need not, nor actors need not, make him say things he did not say and know things he could not possibly have known. I think it unjust and offensive. For example, in a costly production of *The Tempest* some years ago the actor who played Caliban was costumed like an ape and evidently instructed in the art of making ape-like gestures. He was a very good actor and it didn't make much difference, but the fact remains that Charles Darwin was not born until 1809. Caliban had in him something of the downward-tending spirit of the element of water, and Stephano detected in him an 'ancient and fish-like smell'. Similarly about the same time I saw a noted performance of *The Merchant of Venice* in which the actor who played the part of the Prince of Arragon was costumed like a fop and spoke his lines in such an affected way that they were unintelligible. I am willing to admit an Elizabethan disposition to ridicule Spaniards, but this character was a king and his lines do not justify such histrionic malpractice. It offended me also in a most fashionable performance of *Much Ado about Nothing* to see Dogberry utterly spoiled, stuffed out into a monstrosity, brought in on a great and quite unnecessary car and made to talk in an idiotic belching way, his dignity ruined. Dogberry, one must remember, was a man of good manners, was an officer (active constable), a householder, one who knew the law, a rich fellow enough and one that had two gowns and everything handsome about him. (Go to!) I am tired of seeing the drunken scene in *Twelfth Night*, the third scene of the second act, the one in which Dover Wilson found so many witty allusions, played in such a way as to be utterly unintelligible. Sir Toby and Sir Andrew were certainly drunk, but they were not that drunk. I am not particular and am willing for actors to have wide latitude in interpretation. In fact I would follow the good sense, good taste and real knowledge of Shakespeare of Harley Granville-Barker almost slavishly.[7] He says in so many words that he would examine the plays, one after another, in the light of the interpretation Shakespeare designed for them.

I agree with him also when he says,

We cannot begin our research by postulating the principles of the Elizabethan stage. One is tempted to say it had none, was too much of a child of nature to bother about such things.

From this point of view it is possible that the modern stage itself and almost certainly the ornate stage of the nineteenth century have been anachronistic. They have over-staged the plays because they thought that was the way the plays ought to be played, and in so doing have widened the gap between Shakespeare and his audience. Drama is a representative art in time and space and it offers a continuum of presentative and representative features. If one moves toward the presentative end the performance grows more and more like ordinary life and also more and more like the relatively bare Elizabethan stage. In one of the most moving performances of *King Lear* I have ever seen, the director had at his command almost no 'advantages', couldn't stage a respectable snowstorm. He had, however, at his disposal some good actors. Costuming became merely symbolic, lighting poor. Nothing could be spectacular, but he went ahead, and had the lines spoken clearly and well with little space between the actors and the audience. The surprising thing was that Lear, Cordelia and the others were like life. The thing seemed to me to say what Shakespeare must have wanted said. If this has a moral it is that Shakespeare did not, as the kindly Garrick thought, lack art and need assistance.

There is another and larger aspect of Shakespeare and his age that may cause readers and actors to go wrong. Aristotle says in the *Poetics* that drama deals with event, and Shakespeare illustrates the principle.[8] He tells stories on the stage, and suspense is the breath of his nostrils. He never invented plots. Indeed few if any authors did until the eighteenth century. Event was God's affair, and it was man's business to find out God's meaning. History and happenings were the mirror into which man must look in order to see the significance of happenings. Characters, on the other hand, were specialized and not typed or invented. They were not pre-existent. The doctrine of humours and temperaments provided an infinite variety of characters, and the question was, how did the participant in events react to the issues that arose? In other words, characters were inferred from events. It is perhaps innocent enough, considering Shakespeare's imaginative excellence, to speak of his skill in drawing characters, but he did not draw his characters, he inferred them. It may amount to pretty much the same thing, but it warns us against over-emphasizing characters and neglecting the portentous importance of event— suspense, solicitude and disaster or escape.[9] The anachronistic neglect of this principle has been a scourge. Shakespeare's finest characters suffer most. We mentioned the case of Coriolanus above, but Hamlet is the worst sufferer unless it be Brutus.

I am willing to rest the case against ideational anachronism on the way it has treated *Hamlet*. If that play had not had a human appeal as wide as the horizon it would long ago have been tied up tight, pigeon-holed and provided with a narrow, erroneous, classificatory label. Let us use it as an illustration.

If these things are true about Shakespeare and if, as is often said, *Hamlet* is his most broadly significant work, no narrow hypothesis will account for the play and its chief character. Goethe found it the representation of 'the effect of a great action laid upon a soul unfit for the performance of it—an oak tree planted in a costly jar'.[10] Coleridge saw in Hamlet 'an overbalance in the contemplative faculty, one who vacillates from sensibility, and procrastinates from thought, and loses the power of action in the energy of resolve'.[11] The popular belief, probably ineradicable, is that Hamlet was an arch-procrastinator. If a runner on second hesitates too long about the enterprise of stealing third, the sportswriter calls him a Hamlet. In Sir Laurence Olivier's film version of *Hamlet* there is at the beginning a great voice from nowhere in particular that resounds through the theatre with the words: 'This is the story of a man who could not make up his mind.' There is then represented a peculiarly active and perspicacious youth who carries out from scratch and in spite of errors and overwhelming difficulties a great enterprise. Of course Hamlet delays from uncertainty and in order to spur himself on accuses himself of procrastination, but the point is that those are just the things that you and I do. They are merely human, and I do not think that either you or I are free from the liability to make mistakes. However it may be in the popular mind, and however ingeniously Hamlet may be pigeon-holed, the fact remains that he keeps hopping out of the pigeon-holes and indicting us on the grave charge of being human beings and not supermen.

In view of the situation described, it would seem that nothing but a generalization about *Hamlet* on the broadest possible basis will give us satisfaction, and I have one to propose. I do not know how old the concept of man as man is. I mean the concept of man, not as youth or age, king or commoner, or the practitioner of any particular trade or profession, but just as man. It must be very old, but not the oldest, for it includes all its specialities. It perhaps is a product of the thoughtful mind of the Middle Ages. From it seems to come the concept of man as Everyman, Humanum Genus, Mankind, Anthropos, and the pilgrim in *Le pelérinage de la vie humaine*. I do not know a broader concept, and that is the key to the character and career of Hamlet as Everyman.

Hamlet has grown up under the finest princely culture known to the Renaissance and is a university student at the University of Wittenberg. Just before the play opens he has been summoned home to Elsinore by the death of his father. He finds that his uncle Claudius has usurped the kingship and that his mother has made a forbidden marriage with his uncle and has done so with indecent haste. The effect of this on Hamlet is shock as expressed in his first soliloquy: [12]

> O, that this too too solid flesh would melt,
> Thaw and resolve itself into a dew! . . .

We see this young man suffering from natural shock and from frustration. Our most modern psychology tells us that a shock is a very serious matter. It is plain in life, and we do not need Freud to enable us to recognize its power and its danger. Let me illustrate this for you from a French short story I read long ago. It is called 'Garcon, un bock!' which means 'Waiter, bring me another beer!' The narrator sees a hopeless sot who sat all day in a café and consumed one glass of beer after another. When his glass was empty he called for another. The waiter brought it and stacked up the chip on which the empty glass had stood in order to reckon the score. The narrator's curiosity was aroused by the spectacle, and he learned the drunkard's story. It began when as a bright lad he went home for his holidays. His home was paradise to him. His parents were the ideals of all that was gracious and respectable—at least to the outside world. One day the boy playing in the shrubbery overheard perforce a quarrel between his mother and his father, which revealed a horrid situation between them. Both were disloyal to their marriage, and the life the boy had loved was revealed as a sham. He returned to school, but studied no longer, did nothing in life, took to drink and ended sitting in the café in silence except when he broke it to say, 'Garcon, un bock!' We do not need Freud to interpret the events of the story as results of shock. Hamlet's first state of mind may be described as one of shock and helplessness.

The Ghost appears and reveals to Hamlet that his father has been murdered by his uncle and calls upon him to carry through a just revenge. It is not a personal revenge but one that is demanded of him as his father's son, and as the true heir to the crown of Denmark. There is no other way to punish the crime and to save the kingdom. His first state is one of uncertainty. He has only his resolution: [13]

> O all you host of heaven! O earth! What else? . . .

In such a situation Hamlet is beset by doubts. He even suspects that the ghost may be an emissary of the devil attempting to entrap his soul. The visit of the travelling players offers an occasion for action, and Hamlet embraces it uncertainly and as best he can. He forms a plan with the aid of the players by means of which he may test the guilt of the King. This is a clever and sound plan and not a mere device, since it rests on the belief that truth is irresistible and must be believed. He knows that Claudius confronted by the image of his actual deed will betray his guilt.[14]

> I have heard
> That guilty creatures sitting at a play
> Have by the very cunning of the scene
> Been struck so to the soul that presently
> They have proclaim'd their malefactions.

Note that Hamlet has been brought to that practical action by means of self-reproaches. I think we may say that self-reproach is the general habit of sensitive humanity.

In the meantime, doubt still hangs upon Hamlet, and he is uncertain whether the plan is worth trying or not, and whether he can accomplish anything at all. In these circumstances he utters his most famous soliloquy. In this he marks for all mankind what Carlyle called the Centre of Indifference. It has impressed the feelings of humanity so well that it is perhaps the most widely known passage in all Shakespeare.[15]

> To be, or not to be: that is the question. . . .

The plan, however, succeeds, and Hamlet soon has a chance to kill the King while he is at prayer. Hamlet has been much censured for not doing this, and the failure has been set down to him as tragic guilt. I think this is an erroneous criticism and that the play tells us that it is. The King is praying but is not having much luck in appeasing the Lord, but Hamlet does not know this: [16]

> Now might I do it pat, now he is praying.
> And now I'll do't.—And so he goes to heaven;
> And so am I reveng'd. . . .

This is not hatred and mere ferocity. It is an attempt to equalize the revenge with the wrong committed. Justice demanded that the rectification should be equal to the injury. It is one of the most ancient of legal principles. Let me make this clear to you by means of the story of Cutwolfe in Nashe's novel 'Jack Wilton'. Cutwolfe's brother has been murdered and given no chance to make his peace with heaven, and

the duty of vengeance has fallen upon Cutwolfe. He
pursues his victim from city to city and finally confronts him, loaded pistol in hand, in an upper chamber
in Rome. His enemy begs for his life, and Cutwolfe
tells him that, if he will curse God and renounce salvation, his life will be spared. The poor wretch does
this and, when he has cursed God and abjured salvation, Cutwolfe fires the pistol into his mouth, so that
he can never utter a plea for salvation. This un-
pleasant story will at least make clear the Renaissance
doctrine of revenge.

Hamlet cannot in honour take the opportunity
offered by the King at prayer, but he takes the next
opportunity and makes a mistake.[17] Old Polonius is
hidden behind the arras in order to overhear a conversation between Hamlet and the Queen and thus
learn Hamlet's secret. Polonius behind the arras cries,
'What ho! help, help, help!' Hamlet thinks it is the
King and kills Polonius through the curtain. His well-
known remark is: 'How now! A rat? Dead for a ducat,
dead!' And when Hamlet drags Polonius out from
behind the arras he says:

> Thou wretched, rash, intruding fool, farewell!
> I took thee for thy better.

Hamlet makes a mistake, and I should like to caution
you and myself against making mistakes, which are
often costly.

This mistake puts Hamlet in great danger, the King
seeks his life, and to that end Hamlet is sent to England. His attitude is known, and his task becomes
much more difficult. On his way to England he meets
Fortinbras in command of troops, and the spectacle of
the efficiency of the gallant Fortinbras causes Hamlet
to take stock of his own case and to compare himself

bitterly with Fortinbras. He is at the very nadir of his fortunes, and he again berates himself: [18]

> How all occasions do inform against me,
> And spur my dull revenge! . . .
> Now, whether it be
> Bestial oblivion, or some craven scruple
> Of thinking too precisely on the event,—
> A thought which, quartered, hath but one part wisdom
> And ever three parts coward,—I do not know
> Why yet I live to say, 'This thing's to do,'
> Sith I have cause and will and strength and means
> To do't.

Hamlet, like all humanity when it strives to do something hard, lashes himself with his own tongue and keeps himself up to the mark, which is the only way for most of us to succeed. And please note that in this instance Hamlet succeeds:

> O, from this time forth,
> My thoughts be bloody or be nothing worth.

It is indeed true that from this time Hamlet never hesitates again.

Hamlet escapes from his enemies and returns to Elsinore. He is in great danger. Horatio says that the news of what has been done in England must shortly be known to the King, and Hamlet replies,[19]

> It will be short; the interim is mine,
> And a man's life's no more than to say 'One.'

But the final expression of Hamlet's masterly resolution is to be found in a prose passage in a conversation with Horatio.[20] Hamlet and Horatio are awaiting the appearance of the Court in order that the dishonest fencing match may be played between Hamlet and Laertes. Horatio says:

> You will lose this wager, my lord.

Ham. I do not think so; since he went into France, I have been in continual practice. I shall win at the odds. But thou woulds't not think how ill all's here about my heart. But it is no matter.

Hor. Nay, good my lord,—

Ham. It is but foolery; but it is such a kind of gain-giving, as would perhaps trouble a woman.

Hor. If your mind dislike anything obey it. I will forestall their repair hither, and say you are not fit.

Ham. Not a whit; we defy augury. There's a special providence in the fall of a sparrow. If it be now, 'tis not to come; if it be not to come, it will be now; if it be not now, yet will it come; the readiness is all. Since no man has aught of what he leaves, what is't to leave betimes? Let be.

Hamlet goes calmly through the enterprise. He is given his death wound with a poisoned rapier, but with his last breath he slays the King.

In Hamlet therefore I see no special faults or eccentricities. His shortcomings seem honestly to be merely those of humanity, and his virtues those that God has implanted in all human hearts.

If one insists on classifying *Hamlet* as a tragedy, not an important matter, one will see that it is not an Aristotelian tragedy. Hamlet was never proud or successful. His road wound uphill all the way, and his reward for persistence was death. Nor is *Hamlet* a tragedy of character, hamartia, tragic guilt. Hamlet makes some mistakes, as who does not, but to blame him for desiring to kill the King in the right way is ignorant and absurd. Perhaps it is best to say that *Hamlet* is a stoical tragedy. This puts it with the great Hercules plays of Seneca and *Prometheus Vinctus* of Aeschylus, which are not bad company.

The stoical terms of the problem of living, both as recognized in Shakespeare's age and as practically effective in our own, are two. The first of these is the

9

courage to act. All men hesitate to take up arms against a sea of troubles, because fear is instinctive in humanity and protean in its manifestations. All men are therefore prone to hesitation and delay. All the blame laid on Hamlet as a procrastinator rests with equal weight on the shoulders of all men, and so of other proposed shortcomings. People know this, and that is why *Hamlet* lives on in spite of classifiers. Another principle inevitably associated with the necessity of action is this: Man must, having done his best, leave the consequences to God, must learn to be indifferent to what Hamlet calls 'the event'. This struggle to act and to act wisely and to discharge one's duty with some indifference to consequences, is man's typical struggle as an individual; indeed, is the typical struggle of the human race against earthly and worldly environment both now and through eons of time.

CHAPTER VI

FREEDOM

A New Freedom—a Liberty we learned and deepened
to match the broadened life of man in modern
America, restoring to him in very truth the control
of his government, throwing wide all gates of lawful
enterprise, unfettering his energies, and warming the
generous impulses of his heart,—a process of release,
emancipation, and inspiration, full of a breath of life
as sweet and wholesome as the airs that filled the
sails of the caravels of Columbus and gave the promise
and boast of magnificent opportunity in which
America *dare not fail.*—Woodrow Wilson, *A Crossroads to Freedom.*

WE MAY fairly conclude that we as humanists
in the field of language and literature are still
positivistic in our philosophy and may therefore be obliged to operate according to many restrictions. Before, however, we conclude that we are hedged
about with various kinds of harmful limitations and
that lack of intellectual liberty is a bad thing for us,
let us consider freedom as an eternal idea of essential
importance, and, if we decide that it is, let us cite
certain reasons afforded by the new epistemology why
our subject of all subjects should not be narrowed in
its scope and disregarded in its function.

One would admit, to begin with, that there are
various kinds and degrees of freedom. Mediaeval
people, for example, were restricted by social barriers,
supposed to be provided by God in His creation, and

by ecclesiastical dominance to a degree we can hardly realize, since the church was the present and perdurable voice of God. Mediaeval people were taught obedience as a first principle of human behaviour and the spectacle of willing submissiveness presented by them was about as perfect as it could be. But yet they seem to have had the liberty of human existence, the liberty of service, and the liberty of communal action. Within his limits a man of the Middle Ages, whether he belonged to one of the two preferred classes, the church and the feudal aristocracy, or not, had a liberty of art and could work at his trade with some freedom and had moreover participation in the enterprises of his group. Obedience itself brought with it certain liberties to man and seems to have preserved self-respect in limited privileges. His liberties seem, however, not to have been individual. He was like a worker in the hive, so much so that the individual worker tended to disappear in the life of the group. Multiple rather than individual authorship and general anonymity seem to be evidence of this general state.

We say that individualism, or free and independent individual action and thought, made an effective appearance in the Renaissance. There is little reason to doubt this. Indeed, Burckhardt makes it the mainspring of the movement.[1] It seems to have been a different kind of freedom and far more effective than that of the Middle Ages. Ascham in *The Scholemaster* presents the freedom and versatility of ancient Greece as the primary feature of humanistic living and thinks of it in terms of individual eminence:[2]

Athens, by this discipline and good ordering of youth, did breed up, within the circuit of that one city, within the compass of one hundred year, within the memory of one man's life, so many notable captains in war, for worthiness, wisdom, and learning, as be scarce matchable, no, not in the state of Rome, in the compass of those hundred years when it flourished most.

And because I will not only say it, but also prove it, the names of them be these: Miltiades, Themistocles, Xantippus, Pericles, Cimon, Alcibiades, Thrasybulus, Conon, Iphicrates, Xenophon, Timotheus, Theopompus, Demetrius, and divers more; of which every one may justly be spoken that worthy praise which was given to Scipio Africanus, who Cicero doubteth, whether he were more noble captain in war, or more eloquent and wise counsellor in peace. And if ye believe not me, read diligently Aemilius Probus in Latin, and Plutarch in Greek; which two had no cause either to flatter or lie upon any of those which I have recited.

We may at least believe that, in the matter of intellectual freedom, the English Renaissance far surpassed the Middle Ages and that in the succeeding generations it lost or was robbed of its liberty.

Civil liberty and the doctrine of the rights of man were no rare things during the Renaissance and actually had more than their fair share of earnest and able proponents; indeed, in those fields of thought they had an extensive inheritance from the Middle Ages. We know such names as Ockham and Wyclif, but it is sometimes concealed from us that there had been great endowments of ordinary populations with rights and privileges, not only those of common law, but those won by wealth or political advantage by the inhabitants of mediaeval towns and cities. The liberty of the citizen under the law was popular and widespread. The Reformation, itself one of the greatest of the intellectual revolts, produced a varied brood of fearless dissent; such as the Peasants' War, the Anabaptist movement, and many almost forgotten revolts and rebellions. Hard and bold thinking appeared among the Huguenots, especially after St. Bartholo-

mew's Eve, and perhaps nothing more stubborn in its
conviction of the natural rights of man is anywhere
to be found than the vast body of Calvinistic thought.
We might refresh our memories with the writings of
John Knox, Christopher Goodman and John Ponet,
and we may add to them Francis Hotman and the *Vin-
diciae contra Tyrannos*. Perhaps the human spirit has
never ranged more boldly than it did in the work of
Théodore Agrippa d'Aubigné. When we recall that religious heterodoxy was treason during the Renaissance
almost all over Europe and realize the tremendous
social, religious, political and martial power of abso-
lutism in England, France, Spain and large parts of
Germany, we are led to minimize the evidences of the
freedom of thought of the sixteenth century; we wonder that it ever found expression and ignore it because,
in large part, it failed.[3] But failure is merely an in-
cident. There was of course in the Renaissance proper
no such orgy of progressive ideas as marked the decade
of the forties in the seventeenth century, but it is a
mere commonplace to say that the martyrdom of
Henry Barrow, John Greenwood, John Penry and
many others was revenged a hundredfold in the Puri-
tan Rebellion. The triumph of toleration was of course
a long way in the future, but the idea of rational toleration was not absent from the sixteenth century. There
is a broad basis laid for it in Hooker's *Of the Laws
of Ecclesiastical Polity*, but Hooker had to wait for
three-quarters of a century before his own party began
to realize the strength and advantage of his thought.

The intellectual freedom of these fighters for human
liberty, although far more extensive than is ordinarily
thought, does not tell the whole story, and it is another
and I think a less obvious element to which I wish to
direct attention, the freedom of creativity in art and

literature. The area to be searched is the minds of the greatest men, artists like Leonardo and Michael Angelo, and poets and thinkers like Hooker, Bacon and Shakespeare and, with certain specializations, Erasmus, Cardan, Montaigne, Spenser, Cervantes, and others. This manifestation of the liberty of genius is as wide as human life itself and almost as baffling. Perhaps we could agree tentatively that there was a liberty to conceive and a readiness to undertake in these great men of the Renaissance not elsewhere to be found in the history of modern times except in the case of certain men in more limited areas. We may take refuge in the thought that the Renaissance was a happy historical and social accident and say that the Renaissance just happened and that in that age men were somehow greater than they had been before or have been since. But it does not seem profitable or justifiable thus to build for ourselves a fatalistic barrier by means of which we may save ourselves from effort and justify our inferiority. I see no reason why we should not make an attempt, however inadequate and obscurely uttered, to look into these inadequacies, which may after all be due in great measure to recognizable obstructions.

Perhaps we might say that man has an instinct for freedom that flows like the waters of a tide by its natural impulse for gratification and that modern man for various reasons restrains, controls, diverts or impedes it. It would be well, I think, if we could bring the Renaissance to life amongst us, but I have no hope that anybody will act, except individually, on the ideal here expressed, but there is encouragement in the thought that, the barriers once down, human liberty will take care of itself. It will grow in volume and force and rise to any height to which it is permitted to rise. I think the growth of human liberty, especially the liberty to think, rests on an instinct and is not subject to regulation. It might be enlightening, and I think true, to say that the Renaissance mind had fewer self-imposed limitations than subsequent ages have had. In later times men have been disposed to take charge of the universe, whereas the Renaissance was disposed to leave it to God. To a remarkable degree the Renaissance man regarded himself as his own area of activity and, although he generated plenty of ideas for running the world, the age as a whole refused to accept them and refused to be patterned.

In the explanation of the situation we might begin with the greatest limitation of all, a limitation so extensive that, when it had been accepted, it affected the minds and conduct of all men. Historically speaking, the Renaissance may be said to have occurred in a happy time. It had plenty of philosophy, but no absolutely dominant system. Even theology, a little inert, was divided in its control and fought most of its battles individually and usually at the barriers. What has proved the greatest enemy of the particular kind of intellectual freedom that concerns us as humanists, namely, the age or cult of experimental science, was in its infancy, and the universe was still one. It had not been divided into matter and spirit, had not been subjected to classification, and the *De Methodo* of Descartes had not been written. What then was the intellectual position of the Renaissance man?

The Renaissance has been described as a time of transition from mediaeval to modern times, and it has sometimes been forgotten that a time of transition may be a time of intellectual freedom and an earnest search for the truth of existence. Old bonds are loosened and new ones not yet secured. This means that the Renaissance, which was a long period, had its own proper qualities and has a right to independent consideration. It should not be looked at either as the waning of the Middle Ages or as the beginnings of the modern world. What interests us are its freedom to create and its enterprise to undertake.

Inferior in art to Italy, in learning to France and in religion to Germany, the Renaissance in England was influenced by all of these countries and was not so inferior in any area as is sometimes thought. It had skill in art and architecture, a good deal of learning and deep spiritual emotions. It is usually said that the greatest greatness of the English Renaissance was in its literature, especially its drama, and this is no doubt true, but in its variety, zest and sincerity the Renaissance in England was not only great but typical. We have broadened the conceptions of the Renaissance entertained by Dryden and Boileau, Johnson and Gibbon, Winkelmann and Symonds, who followed the opinion entertained by the humanists themselves, namely, that the art, literature and learning of Greece and Rome awoke in the minds of the men of the Renaissance freedom of action, appreciation of beauty and knowledge of the world, and did this by a revelation of the art, architecture, literature and philosophy of the ancients. This is true enough as far as it goes. No one can deny, in the genesis of the Italian Renaissance, the importance of the spectacular revelation of Greek and Roman civilization, but it is not enough. We know now that there were economic and political factors in Italy and elsewhere in Europe that helped in an essential way to establish the new age; also that there were powerful and concordant philosophical influences, such as Neo-Platonism, that helped to promote new thinking in new fields as well as, in Plato's case, some ability to think on the level of the abstract. There were other forces at work that ought not to be forgotten, such as the migration to Italy of Greek scholars after the fall of Constantinople, the European custom of resorting to Italy for study; also explorations and discoveries, and the fostering attitudes of several great kings and courts. But let us understand ourselves. These things are the accidents, no renascence resides in them, and the true origin is yet to seek.

In order to find it let us return to the rather vague statement made above, the idea, namely, that the effective intellectual freedom of the Renaissance was an interim freedom between scholastic rationalism and the age of reason. This would mean that neither of these invaders of man's central kingdom, which is himself, was in a position to exercise domination. It may be pointed out that experimental science itself arose from a revolt against reason but that it resulted in a new set of authoritarian dicta called methods. During the early career of the new rationalism there was a period when the bonds were not so regarded. The tragedy came when men became convinced that their kingdom was divided in two and that man and his mind did not yield to experimental science. As long as science busies itself with objective matters and as long as organized religion concerns itself with theology and worship they do little harm to the creative activities of the human spirit, since they do not oust man from the mastership of his own house. I mean that man as man may be, in a strange and largely unknown way, the master of himself. He lives and moves and has his being in, let us say, a central region that does not yield itself readily, if at all, to scientific investigation on the one side or to effective authoritarian rationalism on the other. When this natural liberty is not interfered with there is nothing to narrow the field and channel the creative mind. In such a situation man may, without prejudice against the many or antipathy to them, be in the best sense individualistic. He lives, be it remembered, in a region that is not investigable by the methods of experimental science. It would follow that the progress of the knowledge of life would be best promoted when man is free to think and speak about himself as a human creature and when he is not interfered with by formalism and authoritarianism, whether self-imposed and voluntarily accepted or imposed from the outside. It is possible that this unusual and seemingly unimportant kind of intellectual freedom was characteristic of the Renaissance to a greater degree than of any other age in the modern world. Man might in such circumstances make great progress in knowledge and understanding of himself, and that he did so in the Renaissance the evidence of the great art of Italy and the great literature of England seem to bear witness.

This is the more surprising and inexplicable when we have made due allowance for the ignorance of the Renaissance, at best an annoying sort of half-baked culture, for the many fetters new and old on the limbs of Renaissance men and women, and for poverty, predation, unfair and unwarranted ranks and classes in society and confusion of ideals and counsels. But, when these allowances have been made, there still remains something actually great in wisdom, insight, sympathy and the revelation of the possibilities of human achievement. Why, we ask ourselves, do the men of that age with all their disadvantages tower over subsequent men of the same races whose opportunities are so obviously superior? It does not greatly help to throw up one's hands and say that renascences in some unknowable way just happen. Surely there are no discoverable differences between the men of the sixteenth century and the men of the twentieth century, or, if there are, they are clearly in our favour; nor, I am convinced, is there any lack of natural ability in the race to which we belong. Neither the bodies nor the minds of men have deteriorated since the sixteenth century. Our opportunities for enlightment are greater by astronomical sums than those of Renaissance people.

It cannot be said that enlightenment surely breeds enlightment. If books, pictures, scholars, sages and artists inevitably produced renascences, we should have distinguished manifestations, for we have access to the whole world. There may be a suggestion of the cause of our barrenness in an imperfectly supported statement sometimes heard that the men of the Renaissance in Italy and the various countries of Europe accomplished what they did because they thought they could; or, as I should put it, because nobody had told them they could not or told them exactly how things ought to be done. In any case, it is far truer to say simply that the men of the Renaissance were not conscious of any limitations of their powers of performance.

Perhaps the customary description of the Renaissance as a period of individualism comes still nearer the truth, and yet the word 'individualism' is loosely used. Perhaps men began to forget the mediaeval faith in the rationality of God's universe and began to take an interest in natural objects and ordinary occurrences for their own sakes. One cannot say that the

individualism of the Renaissance showed any hostility
to collectivism or sought the isolation of the single
human creature from contact with the many. It cannot
have been individualism as we now understand the
term. It was not solipsistic or ordinarily predatory or
was not disposed to displace God or usurp His throne.
I personally think that it was a naturalistic individualism supported by inner and unchallenged freedom.
We have attempted to get closer to the individualism
of the Renaissance by describing it figuratively as in
a central position. I have said that the Cartesian
dichotomy of the world into the material (mistaken
for the real) and the spiritual had as yet not come into
effect. The distinction was old and familiar, but it
had never been taken too seriously or, indeed, understood in its implications. To the Renaissance thinker
the spiritual was merely the material attenuated beyond the reach of the senses. Mind was (and possibly
still is) located throughout the body and not in the
brain alone. It was thought that hands and feet and
organs all had minds, but these very crudities located
all of man in the centre of action and event. The
tablets of scientific method had not been handed down
from a new Sinai, and men were merely and naturally
in the way of great discovery and great understanding
of themselves, their fellowmen and their environment. In such a situation a few errors and oddities
make little difference. Our understanding of nature
and external life as well as of ourselves arose from
within and did not come from the imposition of hypotheses and methods that did not and could not
apply. Whether the axiomatic method of the symbolic
logicians will win acceptance and achieve results I do
not know, but it is at least poles asunder from the
methods of experimental science.

Meantime, human nature and human life, individual or collective, are so far not subject to examination by the scientific method. A true knowledge of what things are and what they do carries with it a knowledge of why things are. It follows that life is an organism of impulse, motive and event and that great students and depicters of life, like Dante and Shakespeare, embody their own methods in their works, or, you may say if you like, that life itself is an operation so inevitably methodized that the intrusion of hypothetical rules and regulations from other areas is error as well as impertinence and that to understand fully the art of the Renaissance, whether that of Leonardo and Michael Angelo or of Shakespeare and Ariosto, is to know both the how and the why. Lord Russell somewhere remarks that it is of little or no importance to ask what electricity is, but of the utmost importance to know what it does. This means immersion in Renaissance art, for from such central place the art and the literature, the wisdom and the brightness of the Renaissance came into being.

The intellectual freedom of the Renaissance was a racial affair, and dissemination throughout a race or community may be an essential of renascence. It cannot, however, be the spirit and activity of a race or community that thinks and moves according to accepted systems and controls, for the self-directed impulse and action of the individual within the social body must be preserved. Therefore when we consider the intellectual freedom of the Renaissance mind from the point of view of our own age and time, we seem faced with defeat from the start. It used to be thought that if our people had political and religious liberty, some degree of financial independence and free access to the best that has been known and thought and done

in the world, a renascence would grow of itself. We
thought that the aspiration planted in the heart of
youth would rise on its own wings; or, to change the
figure, the tables for the feast have been set in ex-
pectation of many guests. When our guests have
proved too busy to come to our feast, we have even
sent out into the highways and hedges to invite in
those who we thought were surely hungry, but our
guests are usually not hungry for the kind of feast we
have sought to spread. The trouble may be that we
have taken over from science and technology a set of
doctrines, now repudiated by the best scientists themselves, that do not and cannot apply to our field of
endeavour. We have preached the freedom of the individual only to find ourselves in a vast and closely
organized society in which millions upon millions of
men and women work under directorates and find
their happiness in so doing. That thirst for beauty,
truth and goodness that we thought was surging up in
every human heart is sadly to seek. We are able to
assess and describe every feature of the Renaissance
except that all-important aspiration toward higher
things, that boldness to undertake and accomplish and
that infinite belief in the powers and capacities of the
human mind. Can it be that, with all our liberty, we
lack the greatest freedom of all, that centrally placed
liberty of man as man?

The hope of a nobler, more effectual and more vir-
tuous culture is not dead, for it can never die. We are
not gods and cannot establish a new order of nature
or of society, but we can refuse to pigeon-hole the ages
and we can come to a better understanding of our
subject. No true philosophy of life can leave out the
important body of judgements, reasonings and depic-
tions that constitute our cultural personalities, and

in spite of many regrettable defections we cannot afford to despair.

The new epistemology, the new logic and the new intellectual freedom at the very top of our cultural pyramid may in the course of generations work great changes even in the vast social, political and racial units of the modern world. After all, even the materially-minded are learning something, and we ourselves are in the way of enlightenment. There are definite things in the new order that may increase our insight and power. We might, for example, reform and rectify our comprehension of the nature of art and our methods of criticism. We might banish classificatory practices, artificial distinctions and mistaken partitions in terms of better and worse. We might acquire truer concepts of fact and its functions and disown our false and outmoded theories of originality and creative art. In other words, we might come into that centre of intellectual freedom occupied transitionally during the Italian Renaissance and learn to see and feel and produce as human beings. By broadening our conceptions of art we might close the breach between art and life and thus render our studies respectable in the eyes of manly men who have something to do in the world.

So far in this chapter we have attempted to present freedom as a general idea universal and, so far as one can see, ultimately potent in its application to the field of thought. Our purpose, however, is specific, namely, the freedom to discover and to give expression to truth even when it runs counter to tradition and authority or to false principles widely accepted as true. The defence or enforcement by any means is dogmatism. The freedom sought is the freedom thought of as essential to progress in all investigation and, in this case, especially in the investigation of discursive subjects, which by definition are unable to make effective use of controlled experiment, the mainstay of the natural sciences. Even there we find the first and fundamental operation is the intelligent examination of particulars. Discursive subjects go that far with the natural sciences in the search for truth, but at a certain variable point scientists can resort to experimental demonstration or to mathematics, and humanists cannot, although they may be, and often have been, as exact in procedure and as determined to find the truth as any scientists. They must in the nature of things follow a different road to the same objective. The scientist in the presence of demonstrated fact tends to become a positivist and possibly did so unchecked until he was told by relativistic philosophy that even his best established principles must be regarded merely as working bases for further search for truth. This put the scientist in the same boat with the humanistic scholar, although there is no doubt that he still has the preferred seat.

But in any case historical and humanistic scholars are by no means helpless. They need not in their search for truth be content with tradition and authority or with mere speculation. One may say briefly that a necessity is laid upon them to examine and understand particulars so thoroughly that significance and inter-relations to the extent necessary to the establishment of the highest possible degree of probability are revealed. This condition has been described rather roughly as the completest possible comprehension— the utmost clarity and plausibility. This, by the way, conforms to the relativistic theory of cognition, which posits a single mental act that provides as part of itself a conception of truth.

My favourite illustration of this is T. W. Baldwin's study of Shakespeare's education. Behind the subject lay an erroneous belief, still widely accepted, that Shakespeare had no formal education.[4] When Baldwin finished his study, there were no more records of Shakespeare's schooling, at Stratford or elsewhere, than there had been when he began, but the totality of the investigation, the soundness of the concept and the agreement of its parts with one another and with the original proposition (that Shakespeare had formal schooling) left no room for reasonable doubt: Shakespeare was educated in an Elizabethan grammar school. There he pursued a course of instruction fully adequate as a basis for his learned culture. No fair-minded reader could deny for one moment the convincing effect of Baldwin's work. Such a painstaking and onerous procedure is, whether we like it or not, the one road to truth in our discursive field.

We shall understand this better and be more willing to accept it, if we consider another simple fact. Literature and the history of literature are a part of human history.[5] Historians of the broader scope never forget that they are, although no doubt the narrowing effects of specialization have caused many historians to be oblivious of the fact and to make little or no use of literary sources and of the power and importance of literature as an age-old human manifestation. In the study of the humanities, on the other hand, there is great advantage in the realization that humanists are also historians of human life on earth and of its characteristics and accomplishments. It lays open to us the procedures and the remarkable progress of history in the modern world. The methods of history are in general suited to our task. We cannot at this time discuss the matter in detail, and it is perhaps sufficient to have called attention to the great successes.

So far the sailing is relatively easy. The difficulty arises when one attempts to enter uncharted waters, but even there navigation is not impossible. One has to resort to logic and epistemology. The approach must be the right one and it must be careful. The general approach we can understand. A bare beginning may be found in argumentation in its original sense. The process was then called the argument from sign, which is really the argument from effect to cause. It is the form of reasoning, usually called induction, that accounts in large measure for the successes of modern history. The argument varies in effectiveness from the finger-print to the broadest of general conclusions. Some epistemologists have rejected induction because of its difficulties and its liability to error. Nevertheless in discursive subjects the argument from effect to cause is a main reliance.

The greatest of these difficulties is the liability to hasty generalization, with the further disastrous liability that imperfect or erroneous generalization may be elevated positivistically into universal and binding laws to be enforced by the full authority of scholars of great reputation and by their less celebrated followers. Symbolic logicians have restated in better and more significant form the principles of correct abstraction.[6] They have vitalized the principle that the context of abstraction must be pure and as complete as possible. This is what logicians had called the intension and the extension of propositions. Since symbolic logic has paved the way to safe abstractions on higher levels of thought, it must be admitted that it has gone a long way towards answering the objections made to inductive procedure. In a field such as that of the humanities, where dealings are perforce with intangibles, symbolic logic opens a clarity in broader comprehension that no scholar or critic in the field can afford to neglect or put aside as inapplicable to his subject. Many of them are specialists narrowly trained, so that to get them even to consider this fact is no easy matter. The principles of symbolic logic do and must apply to humanistic study or we remain victims of every sort of conjecture that ignorance, partisanship or ingenuity can invent.

Simple illustrations are easy to find. The field of Shakespeare study teems with them. Shakespeare, a heaven-born genius and child of nature, had no need of any formal education, and over against that the conflicting idea that no uneducated man could possibly have written the plays, which must therefore have been written by somebody else. Shakespeare was in Stevenson's words a 'sedulous ape' whose skill and greatness were borrowed from his predecessors;[7] instead of his being a man possessed of an originality like that of Bacon, the doctrine of imitation being the moving force. Because *The Contention* and *The True Tragedy* in their present state are full of parallels and even quotations from Greene, Peele, Marlowe and Nashe, the plays in question were written by these dramatists, jointly or severally, and Shakespeare in *Henry VI 1* and *3* merely revised their work. Shakespeare was not a dramatist depicting the impact of event on various human beings; his greatness lay in his delineation of character at large. And so on. But let us take a more immediate case and enquire into it.

About the end of the First World War certain scholars invented what came to be called the bibliographical method.[8] There has rarely been a more hopeful invention. It was immediately in line with, indeed was the adoption of, the inductive principle of procedure in the discovery of truth from effect to cause, the logical method by means of which modern historians have made great progress. It was and is the road to success in all discursive subjects, but it needs to be intelligently followed. Its rules are simple and have been explained above. It observes particulars and attempts to determine their significance in terms of abstraction, a fundamental and omnipresent mental operation. The rules are that the context of generalization shall be pure, that is, must include only members of the projected class—no sheep included in the class of goats. It must also be as complete as possible. Enumerations cannot always be made complete, although sometimes they can and always they must go far enough to achieve probability. It follows that incomplete examination of data (of various kinds) is liable to distort the abstraction.

The first application of the method was to four of Shakespeare's plays of which there are faulty texts. The examination of data had not gone far enough, and the only sound conclusion to be drawn was that these four texts were bad, and that was known before. The attempt to explain the badness of these texts was also a failure, because the context of abstraction was imperfect, since it failed to observe and to give proper weight to the most patent agent of deterioration of all. The authors therefore resorted to plausible speculation and fixed upon the rather attractive idea of the pirate actors. Their followers, dissatisfied with this, changed it to the vague concept of reporting. The subject shall be re-studied with greater care.

Some considerations seem to be adverse. The context of generalization as to the cause of the badness of these texts, as of many others that have been added to the original list of four, may be faulty in the fact that it neglects or fails to perceive the importance of the degenerative effects of acting plays on the stage. This is sometimes merely in the form of necessary and defensible changes made in carrying the written word of the author over into the spoken word of the actor. Elizabethan actors were members of an actors' guild and had a degree of independence unknown to the modern world. The play was theirs by purchase to be spoken as they chose to speak it. Shakespeare was not a classic, and actors took liberties with the text always, sometimes slightly and inoffensively, but sometimes not. Changes would, we may believe, continue to be made when plays were revived. When actors were ignorant or inept, or the troupe was too small, as in provincial companies, where changes were certainly greater and more harmful. But, whatever may have been the special circumstances and causes, the alterations were made and recorded in prompt-books. They are in general easy to identify, and they appear in every text that has been acted on the stage. They constitute, moreover, a continuum from the scarcely noticeable alterations in the text of certain plays, in the gradual increase of change and corruption, to the worst known cases. What has been done is to cut off a certain number of the worst cases and treat them as a separate class, which is an obvious violation of the logic of abstraction. This is not to say that there were not other forces of deterioration, such as the errors of printers, but only that this is the major force.

But the reader might ask, what has this to do with the doctrine of freedom spoken of so earnestly in the earlier parts of this chapter? The answer is that it has a great deal to do with it. Invented causes and general speculations sponsored by celebrated scholars and taught in post-graduate schools to scores of lesser scholars as unshakable eternal truths become the bases of militant dogmatism. To show disbelief in them in toto is unendurable heresy to be resisted fanatically—and effectively. Whatever else this is, and it is a lot of very disagreeable things, it is certainly a restriction and violation of the principle of liberty under the law. Not only that, but the source of it is also an enemy of freedom. This unwarranted, unbecoming and harmful scholastic positivism, possibly taken over from the more justifiable positivism of the old science (although that itself has been condemned), arises from the practice of over-specialization in discursive fields, itself an unfortunate borrowing. A narrow specialist is almost inevitably a positivist. Perhaps he has to be. In his field he must know all the answers, his profession requires that he shall be infallible, and his ignorance of philosophy, logic, history, literatures ancient and modern, even of contiguous parts of his own selected area, ensures his continual narrowness. These matters are settled once for all, and your positivist is bored as well as angered to have them put in question. Again, whatever other disagreeable things might be said about over-specialization in discursive subjects, the fact remains that it is a potent enemy of freedom. We may hope that this positivistic intolerance is a temporary hindrance to progress and that it will diminish with the adoption of a freer as well as a truer epistemology.

CHAPTER VII

THE HISTORY OF AVOIDANCE

So, because it is subjected in the mind of a man, the law of imitation, of resemblance, remains constant for our art, but in a sense purified. It must transpose the secret rules of being in the manner of producing the work, and it must be faithful and exact, in transforming reality according to the laws governing the work to be done, as science in conforming thereto. What it makes must resemble not the material appearance of things, but some one of the hidden significances whose iris God alone sees glittering on the neck of his creatures—and for that very reason it will also resemble the created mind which in its own way discerned those invisible colours. Resemblance, but a *spiritual* resemblance. Realism, if you like, but transcendental realism.—Maritain, *Art and Scholasticism*.

IF ONE reads the quotation at the head of this chapter, one might also read this, which is an anonymous poem in Ravenscroft's *Deuteromelia*:

> We be three poor mariners,
>   Newly come from the seas;
> We spend our lives in jeopardy,
>   While others live at ease;
> Shall we go dance the round, the round,
>   Shall we go dance the round?
> And he that is a bully boy
>   Come pledge me on this ground.
>
> We care not for those martial men
>   That do our states disdain;
> But we care for the merchant men
>   Who do our states maintain;

To them we dance this round, around,
To them we dance this round;
And he that is a bully boy
Come pledge me on this ground.

One would hardly believe that there is any relation between the paragraph and the poem, but there actually is one tiny gleam—almost too small for sight —not narrowed out of existence. Otherwise there is complete inapplicability. How did the poem come to be written? Might it not be well to declare that the thing is not poetry at all and to give oneself shame for being somehow pleased with it?

It is necessary at this point to repeat certain things that have been said in the preceding pages.

The process of cognition has always been a mystery, now dispelled, and has been the mother of superstition. Because men did not understand the enormous capabilities of the human mind and were ignorant of its processes, they resorted to divine intervention either direct or in the form of a superhuman faculty called intuition in order to explain achievements beyond the scope of their comprehension. The new epistemology simply fills the gap and leaves no need or room for supernaturalism and shows that man is capable of works of genius whether he thinks so or not. It provides a conception of Deity so noble that it despises hocus-pocus and favouritism. This superstition lives and flourishes still. Even Bergson and Croce are not entirely free from these traditional bonds. Our literary critics and most minor poets are still defending what one hopes is the last redoubt of superstition. Elizabethans, being fortunately for them pre-Cartesian, were not burdened and hampered by this belief and, in spite of ignorance, witchcraft, intolerance, poverty and error, achieved a renascence of both art and humanity. No such prospects of freedom and progress as those offered by the new theory of cognition have faced the learned world since the age before Descartes, or at least since the exaltation of deduction in the eighteenth and nineteenth centuries, as seem to face it now.

What happened seems to have been this: song, story and commentary became an affair of the educated classes under the direction of mainly dogmatists. There was a body of literary theory inherited in degenerated form from antiquity. This, however, made little difference as long as it was disregarded or unknown to ordinary people. It had come in the form of law and authority and became more and more dependent on publishers and sales. Literature became a specialty, a mystery, that discouraged people who had only natural impulses. Poetry and literature itself were defined and by that means narrowed. In spite of the fact that artistic expression is as broad as life and does not lend itself to positive partitions and classes, it was divided into genres and classified not according to function or any tangible criterion.

The Renaissance had known these rules and regulations and, in such doctrines as that of mimesis and of poetry as a means of pleasant teaching, began the process of robbing ordinary people of a natural means of expression. In the seventeenth and eighteenth centuries title to artistic utterance, oral or written, was pretty thoroughly made over to theorists, and only exceptional naturalists and those of broad and exceptional genius, like John Bunyan, Henry Fielding and Oliver Goldsmith, and they not always, broke through the conventional barriers into a broader world and proceeded in untrammelled freedom. After Dryden and the critics of the Augustan age, there was little hope for freedom, although one remembers with pleasure that literary criticism was mainly authoritarian and was therefore intelligible. Whitehead thinks that Wordsworth and Shelley saw that literature is in essence an expression of life and rebelled against authority, and in his chapter, 'The Romantic Reaction' in *Science and the Modern World*[1] points out the more inclusive attitude of these poets. They of course produced some betterment. By the end of the nineteenth century, however, their broader concepts were perverted or forgotten. Neither poets nor, indeed, the able literary critics of their age gave adequate expression to the principles of the revolt they had led. The case of Wordsworth is interesting, since in his Preface to the *Lyrical Ballads* he seems on the verge of a concept that is adequate to the situation presented by literature and life.[2] The main trouble was that he retained the ancient theory that literature has as its *raison d'être* the giving of pleasure. This of itself caused him to entangle himself in the maze of poetic forms and to make too narrow an application of the idea of situation. As long as he paid deference to the doctrines of traditional poetics, even when he opposed them, he could not assume the completely free position to be inferred from process within the time-space continuum.[3] In the nineteenth century our subject of English literature, not yet fully established as a department of study, did as well as could be expected in a situation in which ordinary people were non-participants and only spectators and buyers of books. Towards the end of that century came our conquest by the scientific method, since when there has been our familiar spectacle of materialistic formalism in specialization along with uncontrolled and irrational empiricism. This is not to deprecate the scientific method but our ignorance and folly in carrying it into fields to the cultivation of which it could not adequately apply and in which it became a narrowing influence of great potency.

The scientific treatment of literature resulted not so much in error as in contraction and diversion. Experience is the only process of understanding in a discursive field such as ours, and the formation of classes in our area is no easy matter. It is not like Aristotle's division into genera and species, which have at hand confirmation by simple examination of fact, and even in the matter of literary forms it is clear that Aristotle classified a definite body of examples in a conventionalized environment. In other words, he did not define and delimit tragedy in general; he presented his observations of Greek tragedy. In the English Renaissance the obsession with forms was already centuries old and had a long history of obstruction and avoidance, but was popularly disregarded until the introduction of science into literature encouraged this still active practice. Schools and coteries make their own metaphysics and thus avoid what is, what has been and what may be—which is the concrete present. Or, as Whitehead puts it: 'It is a world also including the activity of the past [as well as the content of the present], and the limited potentiality of the future, together with the complete world of abstract potentiality, the realm of eternal objects [universals?] which transcends, and finds exemplification in and in comparison with, the actual course of realization.' Contexts of abstraction in fields of such breadth as ours are relativistic and difficult to construct, and the defect was not in the lack of learning and careful thought but in immature generalization, the neglect of the total view, the acceptance of mere conjecture and the driving through and generalization of too narrow hypotheses. When these things become the practices of whole professions they result in general avoidance of experience.

There then began an unwise formalism deductively applied. Our subject was sliced into periods and particularized forms, and specialization in the parts of parts began and has continued to this day. To be just about it, indispensable things were accomplished, mainly of course in the factual regions of our field, by the new group—dictionaries, epitomes, biographies, bibliographies, and such aids to study as the accumulation of materials, the publication of texts, and, for a time at least, the perfection of historiographical techniques. But our subject took on a different kind of interest, lost much of its natural appeal and became the prey of solipsism and the victim of narrow specialization. It sank so low, in fact, that it accepted the theory of a spatially limited concept of the human brain and thought absurdly that a man can know only one thing and that other things take up room in the human head. Obviously they forgot or never knew the estimate of nine thousand million synaptic connections or possibilities of ideation in the human cortex. We were, moreover, overwhelmed with theories, many of which lack not only factual support but any reasonable plausibility. I am suggesting that the positivistic course we have pursued with its narrowing features is coming to an end and that there now appears a new direction.

Certain of the physical sciences are proceeding as if with a new life, and perhaps it would be acknowledged that discursive subjects are not. Indeed, it was the belief that they are not that brought the subject up, and it was natural to ask why, since knowledge is one and there are no insurmountable obstacles in our way. The most general reason for our special lack of progress is that our subject has become a mere department of learning. There is an objection to our being thus set aside, and it is a sound objection. In large areas of the earth we have in our charge the native language and literature of a race or many races. The doctrine of symbolization tells us that the mastery of this language and this literature is not a mere matter of polite culture. It is the way in which the minds of men grow and develop. The fitting of symbol to idea and event is the only process that counts in the progress of intellect. If this is true, teachers of the native language and literature need to know, besides their own great subjects, religion, philosophy, history, science and current affairs, there being simply no limit to what they need to know. Our absorption by a segment of the population, whether commercial, academic or social, has thus helped to rob the people as a whole of their birthright. They no longer sing and have become mere spectators who while away an existence made dull by non-participation. Even their vulgarities are not their own. No renascence of general import can succeed unless it appeals to people as such.

When Whitehead said, 'Reality is just itself', he is asserting the unity of all knowledge and its actuality, and, when Lord Russell asked his famous question, 'If the axioms of mathematics may be accepted as true, why may not axioms or self-evident truths in other areas of experience also be accepted as true?' they opened for us a portal and laid upon us a difficult but essential task, a task moreover not to be accomplished by the multiplication of unsupported theories, hypotheses and speculations, but by the truest and broadest possible observation of experience—the completest possible knowledge of event and inter-relation and the sincerest and most natural emotional reaction. This brings us at once into the realm of induction and re- liance on the natural way in which, from infancy to old age and from savagery to civilization, the mind of man grows and develops, namely, the adjustment of symbols to objects, ideas and events. This is the only road to truth in the vast field of the intangible that we profess to cultivate. For us there is no easy road and there must be no avoidance. We must not be de- terred because wisdom is now out of fashion, for we have no substitute for wisdom. We must make friends with the homely virtues of patience, industry and per- severance. There is no other way. We must again listen for the voice of wisdom and turn a deaf ear to the glib pronunciamentos of mere theory.

But this is not all. The new concept of cognition unifies the process of thought and makes cognition one mental act and not two. It finds no place for super- stition, such as divine intervention in artistic activi- ties, or its substitutes, god-like intuition and super- human genius. This better psychology frees us from dogmatism and makes solipsism childish. Recognition of truth becomes an immediate, although often long delayed, result of cognition itself. This satisfaction in truth, or other eternal ideas, is all we humanists have, and, whether we like it or not, we are forced to accept Bishop Butler's maxim: Probability is the very guide of life.

The new philosophy supplies us with symbolic logic, an indispensable supplement to the traditional dialectic, based on Peano's belated discovery with reference to the copula in the proposition. He saw that the copula often meant, not identity, but 'belongs to the class of'. It so happens that symbolic logic sup-

plies us with an effective instrument for the discovery
of truth in our discursive field. This it does primarily
by its clarification of the process of abstraction. In initial practice this becomes a doctrine of the formation
of classes. It lays down the principle that the context
of generalization or classification must be pure, a
status that careful observation can usually control. It
also says that the context of generalization shall be as
complete as possible—at least to the point of maxi-
mum probability—and this by its very statement lays
upon us the burden of experience.

It is odd that, in a field given over to excessive and
unnecessary classification, classification itself should be
so erroneous. Both symbolic logic and common sense
tell us that the context of an abstraction should be
pure and as complete as possible. No object should be
admitted to a class unless that object has the criteria
of the class under construction. This seems quite
simple, but let us consider the state of our scholarship
as regards so familiar a subject as the early versions of
Shakespeare's plays. There are thirty-seven plays in
the canon, thirty-six of which appear in the folio of
1623. For some of them there are publications of single
plays in quarto form, sometimes two versions separ-
ately so printed, sometimes a good text and a bad text.
The field of obervation is simple enough, but instead
of studying these versions in order to determine in
the light of their markings and, indeed, in the light
of their total relations, how and why they came into
existence and thus classifying them according to actual
fact, scholars have sometimes distributed them according to unsupported conjectures. If there is a special
class of bad quartos, that class must be defined and de-
limited by an exclusive and consistent context. Cur-
rently they are regarded as pirated or as quartos

derived from the process of memorial reconstruction. They have been supported by a series of mnemonic criteria, although, as everybody knows, mnemonic features characterize writing, copying and printing as well as memorizing plays. The context is incomplete, since it omits or neglects the most important criterion of all, which is the alteration and degeneration of plays when put on the stage. Some of these authoritatively supported conjectures may be capable of proof, but so far it is inadequate.[4]

In fact I suggest tentatively that, from ignorance or disregard of these principles, certain defects and errors sometimes accompany our thought, and, even more important, that certain attitudes in need of correction, mainly an unwarranted positivism, involve us in confusion and debate and obstruct our progress. However, since the justification of common sense as an agency in the determination of truth is one of the doctrines of the new epistemology, and since we have not, in general, lacked care and judgement, the problem of correcting vast quantities of error is inevitably a matter of enlightment, and it is in this belief that I wish to be understood. I suggest that our errors arise because of accepted classifications that are mixed or incomplete in the criteria of their contexts. With reference to completeness I suggest that many of our multitudinous scholarly and critical theories and *a priori* speculations violate the ontological principle, since they have no adequate factual support. Owing possibly in some measure to our association with the natural sciences, there has been created in us a classificatory habit, so that our subject is filled with uncoordinated classes and far too many of them. I would even suggest that some of them remain erect by the use of the crutches of the invented cause. It is certain also, possibly because of the haste in which we live, that we sometimes forget or fail to perceive the probative value of the total view, although that is the *sine qua non* of induction, which is our sole initial reliance. The failure to achieve the total view is an ignorant child of specialization. One is disposed to make, not the scientific method, but our unwise adoption of it, the culprit. The scientific method itself is not wrong, its successes show that it is effective, but it does not and cannot apply completely in discursive fields of investigation.

And yet the scientific method, particularly in its restrictive and narrowing analytical tendencies, has in my judgement a lot to answer for. In its very infancy it helped to murder the Renaissance and began the process of putting us in chains. Its main offence is that through the ages it has insisted on defining literature and in so doing has made of it a mere department of learning and not the voice of humanity uttering all forms and phases of life. Under its influence literature became and still remains a mystery, an affair, not of all the people, but of a class. It told us what poetry is and said that, if we wished, just as human beings, to write poetry, we must comply with certain regulations. It was due to our folly that we believed them. Song, story, and drama became formal and definitive things that pertained not to all the people but to a selected few. Our new concept might at least bring forth a doubt as to validity of title and might question the ownership of literature and the production of literature by any special class of people. It may be that literature belongs to the people as a whole and not to professional poets, critics, publishers, reviewers and specialists, and that to get it out of their hands, impossible as that may seem to be, and into the hands of the race is the primary condition of a renascence. The literature of the Restoration and the eighteenth century was restricted in its originality by mere theories. The nineteenth century did not achieve true liberty and the twentieth, with all its empiricism, has made the bondage complete.

Let us think of it for the moment as the intrusion of the intense analytical formalism of the scientific method into the field of literary study, although, because of the relative lateness of the reception of English literature into the *studium generale,* it did not absorb us completely until the end of the nineteenth century. Let us think of it as a deductive procedure *a priori* based on the notion of a pre-existent structure or temple of art and learning designed by the Almighty and to be gradualy constructed according to pattern by succeeding generations of human builders. This prefigures what I have called positivism. The simple fact is that the relativists say that the cosmos is not like that and that its process and intelligibility are of a different sort. My interest is not in this issue but in a certain freedom that is promised us and in a thorough-going readjustment of formalism in the study of our subject. The traditional conception of learning is now abandoned by the leading philosophers of science of our time, who regard so-called principles as merely working bases for further search for truth. The Cartesian dichotomy of reality into matter and spirit, or rather the identification of matter with reality, has gone by the board, and one notes with some surprise that neither physics nor biology is now materialistic. With us processes should be reconceived, and scholarship and criticism be recognized as merely differing aspects of one search for truth. The world of Homer, Sophocles, Petrarch, Chaucer, Mon-

taigne and Shakespeare did well enough without partitions and rules, and so might we if we could get rid
of them or learn to ignore them.

There is a sort of stiff-mindedness that goes not only
with extreme subservience to authority but with the
scientific approach to discursive subjects. A new idea,
like the Keynes discovery of the economic effects of
the cheapening of money, has not been integrated
with what is already known but is taken as superses-
sive of all that has been learned. Every problem is
thought of as single and to be solved by a discovery,
and every issue that arises within the limits of a theory
is blindly subsumed under it. For example, the theory
of textual criticism is not only an effectual but a
liberal system that makes provision for all special conditions that appear in the sequence of classical texts.
But, when the doctrines of classical textual criticism
are applied unthinkingly to mediaeval and Elizabethan dramatic texts, they do not always fit. Differences
and variants came about in other ways than sequen-
tial copying and printing. If such interferences with
normal sequence had appeared in the history of classical texts, allowance would have been made for them.
The matter has some importance, since if there is a
question as to whether the folio text or a quarto text
of a Shakespearean play is the substantive text and
the issue is settled wrongly, the text in question is
vitiated. One cannot attribute to Elizabethan publishers the meticulous exactitude of modern scholarship. Indeed, it is anachronistic to do so. But Elizabethan compositors did make common-sense corrections
in the texts they printed and reprinted. To conclude
that a given reprinted quarto that has had some simple
corrections at the hands of a competent compositor
was used as copy for the folio text is in the circum-

stances doubtful. The original readings may have lain undisturbed in an official playbook and were merely restored by the printer. To add to that the conjecture that the quarto has been collated with a quarto playhouse copy seems to be an invented cause. Scholars also sometimes proceed on a basis of mere identity and disregard Lachmann's discovery of the significance of common error.[5]

By broadening the field it is possible to make the error-breeding effects of formalism more evident. The general error may be described as dogmatism playing into the hands of avoidance. One may also say again that in practice acceptance rests on experience. Shakespeare, for example, made his way to fame mainly because larger and larger numbers of people by reading his plays and seeing them acted became convinced of his greatness. Critics were not only hostile but authoritative. Shakespeare succeeded, not by the assistance of critics, but in spite of their hostility, and it took him a century and a half to do so. This is also true of Milton and is a mere commonplace. It has present interest mainly because in altered form it is a still continuing condition, although it is probable that what might be described as avoidance has taken the place of authority.

Shakespeare is not mere entertainment and pastime. He, when he has his way, compels his students to confront life in ways often demanding thought, respect for truth and courage. Because of the fact that this deeper significance, deeper insight, deeper and truer instinct for truth and wisdom in Shakespeare are actually the basis of his greatness and the foundation of his acceptance by the world, these things make demands that even famous critics reject and seek to avoid.

This avoidance takes many forms: Shakespeare is

mere amusement, mere fine art, let us submerge ourselves in dramatic or theatrical art. Let us devote ourselves to images without troubling ourselves to know
anything about symbols. Let us avoid event and remain ignorant of the fact that Aristotle, in the *Poetics*
itself, says that drama is concerned primarily with
event. By devoting ourselves solely to character we
can avoid life and proceed in the belief that characters
are typed and that Shakespeare selected them cate-
gorically, and thus avoid the thought that human character is infinite in its variety, for we might find it
troublesome to ask, as Shakespeare plainly does, what
sort of characters we ourselves are responsible for.
Shakespeare's greatness is an appeal to sincerity, and
sincerity is laborious and troublesome to many critics.
We may thus avoid Shakespeare and win a happy success by taking refuge from Shakespeare in avoidance
or solipsism.[6]

The fallacies, avoidances and erroneous classifications of current English scholarship ought to be easy
to correct, since the great body of research in the
humanities is sound and sensible. What we are now
doing to extend the bounds of knowledge and correct
the errors of our predecessors is altogether praise-
worthy, and with a truer epistemology will go forward
with increased energy and intelligence. My point is
that it is not enough, not adequate to the demands
laid upon us in the field of English language and
literature.

In a world filled with such abundance of knowledge
and such variety of things for many reasons worth
knowing, the resort to epitomes and commentaries is
natural enough and in a certain sense practical or even
necessary, but, if it supersedes and obscures the actual,
it affects adversely the intellect and originality of an

age. Ages like the Alexandrian and large parts of the Middle Ages that have contented themselves with epitomes, selections and encyclopaedias, although possibly prosperous, have been dull and unoriginal. It may be that that fate impends over discursive areas in our own epoch. We often learn, when we do learn, at second-hand from digests and descriptions of subjects. We have at best variously selected samples. Indeed, there is a large and influential body of specialists in education who advocate curricula made up of descriptions and epitomes of subjects chosen for what are thought to be utilitarian ends, which in the long run obscure the originals. Epitomes and digests are, however, apparently found useful to students confronted by the necessity of passing examinations and are sold in large numbers. In our subject there are outlines of the history of literature that provide not only names, dates and brief biographies of authors and précis of literary works, but provide also commentaries in brief form that tell the student what he had better think about them.

These things must in our systems serve very well, since they are teaching devices and, if one's reliance is on teaching rather than learning, they are certainly justifiable. They present a corpus of instruction and reveal what is being taught, namely, information about books and what to say about them and not the books themselves. For purposes of passing tests and amassing credits toward requirements for degrees these brief compendia no doubt serve extremely well. They reflect lectures and text-books of very good grade, and if mere completion of courses of study and standards of graduation with, of course, social advantages, are the object of going to colleges and universities, there is nothing much to be said against them.

Teaching by teachers and not learning by students has come to be an established practice in American institutions. It was becoming customary in Woodrow Wilson's time. He objected to it, and tried, with some temporary and local success, to substitute learning for teaching in the institution over which he presided. He certainly regarded the education of every individual as strictly dependent on what that individual did for himself and thought of the teacher as an adviser of the student and as a companion of the student in the process of learning. I remember that he said on one occasion that university lectures should not be used to convey information, which should be gained from books. Lectures might, he said, be useful and time-saving in the presentation of total views of areas of knowledge, also as exemplary demonstrations of how creative and expository tasks should be carried through. He was in doubt as to the value of lectures designed to inspire students to greater effort.

In my time at Oxford the English seemed to have little reliance on anything except the efforts of students themselves, although, as I recall, private tutoring, often by experts, was in very common use. I think, however, that tutors served in some degree as energizing agents and that the English adhered to what seems to be the only sensible policy; that is, that personal effort by the student in actual contact with the subject studied is the only basis of education. I am not informed on current British practices and theories of education, but, to judge by published criticism and research, it may be that the British have been to some degree affected by specialization, dogmatism and educational short-cuts.

No doubt the two aspects of education, teaching and learning, form a continuum in which by intelligent adjustment a proper balance in practice could be worked out, but to exaggerate teaching to the neglect of learning in higher education is to institute an almost fatal condition of avoidance. What great literature does by actual experience is to instruct, breed the habit of individual reflection, provide patterns of action and develop character. Frankly, there is no inspiration or any other human value in reading a synopsis of *Iliad* or *Paradise Lost* compared to reading those works themselves.

To the extent to which systems establish descriptive procedure based on mere commentary and summary instead of experience they act as screens against the actual, and they fail. If experience of the actual is the only basis of education, one cannot say that, except for social ends and personal vanities, teaching by means of generalizations made by somebody else has much in its favour. This subject is worth considering, since the same habits of shallow routine appear in criticism and even in so-called scholarship. Such formalized, stabilized, and essentially lifeless procedure robs the student of a chance to know, appreciate and benefit by the works and subjects selected for his study. Of course the student will have to work possibly as hard as his teachers do, but he ought to learn from those responsible for his education that there is no education possible in this world without work. Who would believe, for example, that merely classifying Tennyson or Shakespeare or Euripides as a poet of a certain kind or grade, assessing the value of his work or even displaying examples of it is comparable to knowing at first hand and by reflection the greatness of his work as a poet and as a source of enlightment and enjoyment? This specious or seeming knowledge, poor as it is, does not belong to the student but to somebody else. The student has nothing of his own. It is moreover, comparatively speaking, very boring and may rob him of the chance to develop a mind and character of his own—actually may cost him his salvation.

There is finally in this country a strongly based movement to make avoidance official. It means decay or deep injury to humanistic study and should be given careful thought, whether such thought is effective or not. I refer to the supersession of direct reading and study by radio and television. Many important institutions of higher education have introduced these devices as a teaching method, and there have been grants by government and by great foundations for its establishment.

The following is from a paper read by Professor Elizabeth Rose of New York University at a meeting of the National Council of Teachers of English at a recent meeting at Detroit:

Some rather startling figures about our reading public have come to me recently. I hear that 75 per cent of our adults read no books, 25 per cent read one book a year, and only 1 per cent read as many as five books a year. . . .

The children of our great unread non-reading former students are now in our schools—in a different world from the one their sparse-reading parents grew up in; a world in which reading meets stronger competition than ever before from other mass media of communication. I live in a city apartment that looks out upon the windows of other apartments facing a courtyard. I can look out my rear window and observe life going on in other windows—and frequently I do—though I have not yet seen a murder. My favourite window is that which frames a family in which there are two young children, four and six; I know their ages and their names, for they come out in the courtyard on a summer day and talk up to me at my window. These small boys have *two* television sets, with which they spend most of their late afternoons and winter evenings. As yet, and I have looked closely, I have not seen a book on a shelf—nor have I ever seen either of their two young parents lift a child on a knee to read him a story. These children *look* and *look* and *look*—but they are never read to. I have given this illustration, not because I think we can generalize from this one family, but because I believe the situation I have described is rather general. . . .

The situation described here is not new. Our people, mainly of peasant stock with backgrounds of illiteracy extending backwards for untold milleniums, have never been readers. The classes who read books have always been a small, carefully fostered and largely self-selected few. All of us believe that the numbers of this class relative to the uncultivated class could be increased, and we find ourselves extremely uneasy for fear, in the diversions of the current world, the reading class is actually losing ground. That means perhaps that in the field of the highest culture American state-supported public education, if not a failure, is a disappointment. We had thought naïvely that the illiterate were pining for the opportunities we enjoyed, and some of them were; but, as a whole, they have displayed not only indifference but great resourcefulness in escaping from the ministrations of bookmen, scholars and teachers. We literary people are not the only ones who suffer. The whole group of arts and sciences suffers in somewhat the same way. Whenever they leave the narrow field of the practical, their followers grow as few as ours. I borrow a motto for this prevalent American class from Hoby's translation of Castiglione's *Courtier: I will not know the thing that toucheth me not.*[7] But I believe that that class is permeable, and it is a chief satisfaction of my life that I have made so many inroads on it. Do not make any mistake. This class in our country is organized and aggressive and many of them occupy the seats of the mighty.

I wish also to remark on Miss Rose's brilliantly chosen words: 'These children *look* and *look* and *look*.' That is, they live in a world of sense impression only, without thought or time to think. This practice is not only almost valueless as a cultural exercise but is intellectually harmful. It wrecks voluntary attention, splinters it, chops it into bits and for that reason prevents the development of character and personality. Character and personality depend on two things, continuity and voluntary exercise, and these two things are almost entirely wanting in radio and television. They both carry sense impression far beyond the bounds of its legitimate function. Woodrow Wilson used to say that instruction was useless unless the recipient mind did something with the information imparted, integrated it with the contents of the mind, accepted or rejected it or took some action because of it. He used to say that the process of giving out facts and systems and requiring them to be given back undamaged and unchanged on an examination paper was an act of intellection, but he thought it the lowest form of mental exercise. We should get it into our heads that the only thing that fosters culture and builds character, personality and mind is what we ourselves do and not what we see and hear and have poured into us. Learning, not teaching or watching or hearing, is the only effective line of action. Therefore radio and television, though innocent enough as convenience, advertising, diversion and amusement, lack the essentials of the educational process.

But not so reading. Civilized culture in any recognizable form came in with it. So far as I can see it has not been replaced. It has been supplemented by the laboratory, the atelier, the directed spoken word, and other inventions, but it has as yet not been supplanted, and there are reasons for this.

The most obvious of references are to ourselves and to our own mental tools, and for most men this fact of obsession with self constitutes a terminal point no less effective than the theological prohibitions of the Middle Ages or the ideological prohibitions of the modern communistic state. It is, however, a well-known fact that, as the ability to communicate grows in the individual and in society, accuracy, directness and completeness are more and more achieved. Originality continues to sprout and spread. Words, by connecting things really but not obviously related, generate new ideas, and such connections are very largely the discoveries of science and philosophy. Communication in its various forms controls much of our mental life and of our actions, but a certain ability in generalization beyond the limits of our immediate selves is necessary if we are ever to be greatly influenced by any communication. Indeed, it is possible that the striking new methods of communication, with their mechanical compulsions to clarity, may bring about changes and possibly improvements in language and literature; but so far their ideal has been the spoken word and the seeing eye, and they lack the universality of appeal of written language. Written language speaks to eye as well as ear and by suggestion to all the senses and does so under conditions that provide time for reflection. The invention of writing and of the printed book seems still deeply entrenched in the process of human culture. No appeal to the eye alone and no reproduction of oral discourse can as yet take the place of the written word. Written language has a universality, a convenience, an economy, and the possibility of leisurely repetition that all of its rivals so far lack. The main agent in reading is the eye, the coolest and most intelligent of the senses, and in the process of reading there is a constant infusion not only of visual elements, but of aural and physiological elements as well, that gives reading an organization like life itself, especially since reading affords leisure for the intermixture of experience and acquired learning. The reading habit still takes hold even in the midst of current distractions. Great books, according to Lord Grey in the *Fallodon Papers*, help us to live better, attune us to the nature of which we are a part, and make us know ourselves as parts of the scheme of things, as children of God and brothers and sisters of men.[8] They make us willing to be friends with ourselves.

What is it then that reading does that nothing else so far in our civilization can do so well? Obviously it affords time for reflection and the voluntary freedom of its exercise provides an invitation and an opportunity to think. For purposes of further definition let us borrow a phrase from A. N. Whitehead. He speaks of *the habit of thoughtful elucidation*. And he adds, 'the autonomy of thought is strictly limited, often negligible, generally beyond the threshold of consciousness'. In order to enrich this concept let us quote a paragraph from *Adventures of Ideas*:[9]

Our consciousness does not initiate our modes of functioning. We awake to find ourselves engaged in process, immersed in satisfactions and dissatisfactions, and actively modifying, either by intensification or by attenuation, or by the introduction of novel purposes. This primary procedure which is presupposed in consciousness I will term Instinct. It is the mode of experience directly arising out of the urge of inheritance, individual and environmental. Also, after instinct and intellectual ferment have done their work, there is a decision which determines the mode of coalescence of instinct with intelligence. I will term this factor Wisdom. It is the function of wisdom to act as a modifying agency on the intellectual ferment so as to produce a self-determined issue from the given conditions. Thus for the purpose of understanding social institutions, this crude threefold division of human nature is required: Instinct, Intelligence, Wisdom.

Returning, however, to the plain fact that reading gives time and affords invitation to thought—both reflective and immediately practical—we find something further to say that both confirms the soundness of the position taken and opens a new vista of incredible importance. It is a discovery of the newest mental science and has to do with the solutions of the problem of cognition or creativity. It has been explained above. You may not have observed some significant features of the process; namely, it is automatic, immediate and carries at the instant what might be called an impulse or incitement to action, change, orientation or enlightment. Creativity turns out to be an affair of the moment. Its incipiency is, to be sure, slight, but the discovery (or new channel in the brain) will, if given time and attention, grow into its full status of importance. Creativity is not, it seems, something that visits the mind suddenly and from nowhere in particular. It is germinated and cultivated, whether consciously or not, within the mind. Wordsworth defined it significantly as 'emotion recollected in tranquillity'.

It is easy to see what increased and genuine importance this idea lends to reading, which, so far, is the most effective device at our disposal for learning to think and for generating new thoughts. It is not too much to say that the written word has created the most enduring features of our civilization, saved it from extinction and built it up to greater virtue and strength. I am disposed to reject spurious substitutes, such as radio and television, and to assign them to the regions of utility and amusement where they belong. I shall stick to the written word until some better device appears for the transmutation of fact and knowledge into wisdom.

It is surprising and most frustrating to observe how fundamental errors live on from generation to generation and from age to age in the great fields of human thought, such as religion, philosophy, medicine and humanistic culture, live on in spite of the advancement of science and the mastery and dissemination of truth. Such ideas are those of the formalized belief in specific cures by doctors, the conception of God as an uncontrolled and uncontrollable tyrant in religion, the faith in mere business among economists, and the complete reliance on teaching instead of learning in the field of education. Society simply does not seem able to detect the fallacies in these things and to modify or discard these deep and hoary errors. They, however, serve to introduce an aspect of the field of reading and of the function and use of libraries.

It is no doubt most helpful to know as much about life as possible, but nobody can comprehend life completely and to spend one's time trying to do so is futile. The thing to do with life is to live it. Now it happens that nearly all the books in a library are about life, and the same principle applies to books that applies to life. Let us define literature as the written record of life, and it will follow that literature, like life, ought to be experienced. Literature, like life, is thus both a subject-matter and a method. You may say if you like that literature both underlies and teaches its own method. Therefore it is tautological, superrogatory and absurd to talk about methods of studying and producing literature, or one may say at least that the methodology of literature is merely secondary and is at best merely ancillary to the main purpose. The main purpose in this connection is reading or experiencing literature.

But what do we find? We find our world of highly trained teachers of literature and proponents of literary culture spending their time on so-called techniques, on classifications, on conventional distinctions, and on discriminations between good and bad literature in spite of the fact that one man's meat is another man's poison. They spend their time on what is called criticism, and this they elevate into a complete and independent subject. This is innocent enough, but it is narrowing in its effect and comes to have little or no valid connection with literature and therefore with life. It would be fairer to say that criticism is one aspect of reading and that to give it extreme attention is to commit the fallacy of mistaking a part for the whole. Or one might say quite simply and sensibly that the critic of literature should know and understand literature itself or he has no useful function.

In our mathematical age we should know more about universals and how to handle them than we do. A library is as varied as life itself. It plays no favourites. But we academicians, faced with infinite variety, proceed too often as if we were dealing with finite numbers. We work within unjustifiable partitions and narrow our minds accordingly. In so doing we are, consciously or unconsciously, guilty of avoidance.

CHAPTER VIII

SCHOLARSHIP AND CRITICISM

> For philosophy, far the most important thing about the theory of relativity is the abolition of the one cosmic time and the one persistent space, and the substitution of space-time in place of both. This is a change of quite enormous importance, because it alters fundamentally our notion of the structure of the physical world, and has, I think, repercussions in psychology. It would be useless, in our day, to talk about philosophy without explaining this matter.— Lord Russell, *An Outline of Philosophy.*

THE RELATION between scholarship and criticism is not difficult to understand, although the new philosophy applied to that relation introduces a few not difficult technical terms. It is the more easily comprehended because the new epistemology restores an original and natural concept. This explanation would no doubt be done with greater authenticity by a philosopher who knew literature if one could be found. Our era of narrow specialization forbids a scholar who professes literature to enter the field of philosophy, or even to look over the fence. But the matter is important, and somebody who understands it ought to make it clear. Since this is true, one hopes that one having only a layman's knowledge of philosophy will not be regarded as an ignorant intruder in the field. In any case, what is about to be said is a strictly literary matter.

The generally accepted theory of cognition rests on the concept of a four-dimensional space-time continuum and declares that cognition itself is a mental activity in the fourth dimension; and it recognizes that, as our minds are constituted, the operation, although actual, is not as a process within the comprehension of our minds. We have spoken above of the mystery of cognition, now dispelled, and of certain opinions in the form of superstition and mysticism that have played a part in the history of literature as well as of thought. These are probably to be regarded as attempts to explain the inexplicable. We are now confronted by questions at issue between scholarship and criticism as now understood. These issues have arisen, not from the terms as originally and fully accepted, but from an unjustified narrowing of both terms.

If we understand by definition that in cognition certain related elements of the space-time continuum meet, let us say vaguely at the focus of consciousness, and an act of cognition takes place in the fourth dimension. The operation itself is unintelligible, but the result is, as I understand the matter, understandable. It may be a recognition, a memory, an association or what not. It is in any case a judgement and it assumes the nature of an entity.[1] It may itself become a factor in other cognitive operations. As an entity, it is analyzable and may be judged as to its validity. This would seem to be the basal operation of criticism. So conceived, it is a responsible operation. It must, as they say, obey the ontological principle, which is another way of saying that it must recognize the truth either directly or by the detection of error. This must be the concept of those who have regarded criticism as of fundamental importance in the advancement of learning both general and individual.

Scholarship is an organized effort to do the same

things—to search for truth, to recognize it as fully and perfectly as possible, and to detect and discard error. Since originally and basally scholarship and criticism have the same purpose, use the same methods, and differ only in limitation of fields and degree of conscious purpose, they seem to be, at least in intellectual activity, one and the same thing with no basis of disagreement and every reason for effective and harmonious co-operation.

But certain things have, in the course of time, happened to these two terms and the greatest aberrations have befallen criticism; scholarship has merely been narrowed in scope. The neo-classicists made criticism the policeman of pseudo-Aristotelian authority. Coleridge and his followers warped it so that it referred to literary appreciation only. Aesthetic ideas were the only ones among eternal ideas with which criticism was concerned. This led to an association of criticism with the ancient superstition that works of genius are the result of revelation or of the kindred form in which great art is produced by superhuman genius, a genius or 'intuition' itself inexplicable in terms of human life. This in turn becomes the organic theory of art, a construction with its own metaphysics in which there is neither cosmology, ontology nor epistemology. One speaks thus impolitely of it, because this theory is at the present time the greatest enemy to the establishment of a natural and sensible idea of the true function of criticism. Some hope, however, appears in the fact that in our time the common sense of ordinary people is affording us a great deal of sound reviewing and some organic criticism that tells what authors say and mean and how they present it. Meantime the poor word has had to afford shelter for empiricists, solipsists and fanatics.

A result of this manhandling of the denotation of the word 'criticism' has had a narrowing effect on the conception of scholarship and made it apply more and more to the discovery and assessment of fact only. This distortion is particularly characteristic of the twentieth century. It is a misfortune, since scholarship in the popular mind is merely and solely the search for truth and has no special commitment to beauty or any other active eternal idea. It should seek truth whether of fact or of interpretation, whether concerned with tangible entities or with thought on high levels of abstraction. Without emotion it is a dead thing without life or driving force.

Again one finds hope in the fact that scholars in all ages have exemplified every kind of breadth and comprehensiveness. The great scholars of the nineteenth century had these things, and even now great scholars get through the narrow gate of specialization and function as fair and appreciative critics. This is the more noteworthy in view of the disappearance of the classics, history and philosophy from the curricula of education in our world. The thing needed is a release from bondage and an amplification of the mind. The same thing is true of those who practice literary criticism, some of whom know what they are talking about and are really good scholars. So therefore we may yet escape from inane fragmentation. The common sense of ordinary human beings may yet prevail.

In the original state there was no conflict between scholarship and criticism, although there may have been and probably was a variation in emphasis. One group perhaps leaned towards fact and its significance and another towards appreciation and enjoyment. These tendencies are certainly universal, and it seems likely that we have to do with a continuum made up among other things of two manifest features, the one, we will say, more interested in the discovery of fact, the other of aesthetic pleasure, the second being the more emotional of the two. There is nothing strange or puzzling about this, for almost every concept if it is at all communal or general presents variation within its continuity.

The continuum suggested here presents no gradual and ordered growth in size and importance, but the fact is that it can be conceived of as a series in which one quality increases as the other decreases.[2] If we thought of it as a piece of paper in the form of a narrow parallelogram with a line drawn from the upper right-hand corner to the lower left-hand corner, the triangle at the top might represent one element and the one at the bottom might represent the other. If you tore the parallelogram perpendicularly through the middle, you would find a perfect balance of the two elements. This might be thought of as a normal and efficient state. If you tore along a vertical line closer to one end than the other, the areas would show prevalence of one element or the other. The one thing you cannot do without destroying the basal concept is to tear the paper along the diagonal line. This crude illustration may enable one to understand certain things about the continuum as a whole. It is of course made up of many elements, but we have reduced it to two. The attempt is to express a total concept, no part of which can be dispensed with or regarded as anything more than a part. If this carries any meaning at all, it is that a scholarship that neglects everything but fact and a criticism that ignores or distorts fact are both unnatural and inadequate in their operation.

But there is no need for all this. What we need are scholars and critics who are willing to be human beings with adequate learning, sound judgement and a sense of the whole, and we have such persons and need more. I am not taking this out of any book or deducing it from any abstruse and more or less incomprehensible philosophy. I am speaking of what I know and have seen and observed. Mark H. Liddell showed me a note-book he had used in a course in Germanic philology under Julius Zupitza. The book was a record of the science of philology, but it was filled with commentary on related subjects—literary values, historic and philosophic interpretation and wisdom in the conduct of life. Samuel Ross Winans's course in the Greek Anthology was in fact a course in all poetry and his course in the *Memorabilia* of Xenophon brought Socrates to life. Bliss Perry, who was thought of as a critic, was notoriously careful of his facts and of the circumstances and special meanings of literary production. The same things were true of Sir Walter Raleigh. Henry Bradley, a great philologist, was all-told the wisest and most broadly learned man I ever encountered. And so on with other great scholars and great critics with whom I have had contact or whose works I know. Whether what I have said about the historical relations between scholarship and criticism is true or not, the fact is that the study of the broadly discursive fields of language and literature demands breadth of view and actual experience and will yield its value on no other terms.

Bacon had insisted on the necessity of experiment, and his teachings, very influential in England,[3] were of course re-enforced and given a new direction as the philosophy of Descartes gained acceptance. Bacon has been blamed for not being more narrowly scientific than he was, although his broader teachings were valid after two hundred and fifty years. It is fair to connect this with the growth of criticism, or, one might say, the continuance of dogmatic criticism. The role of authoritarian criticism was augmented in the later seventeenth century and it became, and has remained, an end in itself, a special subject with its own so-called principles. Its view, except in the case of the greatest critics, has been dogmatic positivism. It is possible that criticism as a subject and not an inevitable part of thought or cognition is a figment of the mind and has no adequate reason for existence and that there is one process and not two; that is, cognition only, not cognition plus super-human inspiration.

Criticism means literally and originally the passing of judgement and as such it is an end-product of cognition. It had, by the seventeenth century, long outgrown its simple meaning and in Aristotelianism had had a long career of its own. It was strictly *a priori* in its approach. This of itself is, in a discursive field, a vice. Setting aside the absurdity of making one factor in thought or cognition supreme, as this exaltation of criticism did, we may admit that it was only good manners and good business for critics to become expositors of the products of art. Such an exercise is commendable, since it might enlighten the critics themselves. Such an operation is not, however, criticism in the original sense, which would mean a return to a natural process in the discovery of truth and beauty. Such critics as Dryden were sincere and, if not blocked by superior authority, might have justified the formal criticism of the seventeenth and eighteenth centuries; indeed, might justify criticism now.[4]

But when criticism narrows the field of artistic effort, organizes its beliefs into formal codes, invents a metaphysics of its own, it becomes a narrowing agent in the field and consequently a harmful influence on literature and literary originality. Critics, whether sheltered behind authority or not, have no right to tell us (and by social compulsion compel us to accept) what the expressive activities of humanity shall be or what parts or aspects shall be in exclusive use as the subject matter of poetry and prose; or, indeed, to dictate what form shall be in exclusive use.[5] The thing still goes on and the total effect has been to discourage artistic effort and expression and to make the mass of people into spectators, whereas they might, given freedom, have become participants in giving voice to themselves and their ages.

But criticism, intellectual fragment that it has come to be, has no right to dispense with knowledge of the object or objects under trial, or to neglect the purpose or the adequacy of the author under consideration. At best it has merely said that the work has or has not complied with some formal technique or style or standards.[6] Even that position would have been intelligible if not justifiable. But regarding itself as an independent art, criticism has gone far beyond this simple dogmatism. It became solipsistic, and the world has been asked to concern itself with the reflections aroused in the mind of the critic by works or groups of works. This in nine cases out of ten is to enter the field of fiction. Criticism must not forget that it is fundamentally the final act of cognition in a psychological process. This confusion has in some measure arisen because literature mistook itself for science. In the prison in which literature is now confined there is a sort of justice, since in the last phase it has suffered itself to become a speciality and a commercial product.

If the foregoing discussion follows the line of truth, those of us who are interested in the future of our subject have at least two questions before us. The first of these refers to our own bailiwick. The opinion has been expressed above that our present approach is often wrong epistemologically. Our initial approach, it has been argued, and our main hope, is by way of experience, primarily inductive or *a posteriori* and not *a priori* or deductive in its method. Reasons have been given why this is necessarily so. What we have to dread is ill-based authority and a merely conjectural procedure, both of which are positivistic in their attitude and end in dogmatism and in avoidance of experience in favour of second-hand commentary—conjectures and so-called principles in the making of which we have had no part, what has been said about literature and not literature itself, so that it is bad form to say anything that has not been said before. Since this is a matter of logic as well as conjecture and since we now have at hand a logic of perfect applicability, we may probably count on an ultimate discovery of a better epistemology and its adoption by scholars in our field; that is, after many deaths and retirements.

The second question has to do with the spirit of the age, and our ability to form or correct that spirit is limited in well-known ways, but it is by no means negligible. Society is governed in this matter by fashion, and fashion changes for the better as well as for the worse; often quickly. It is at least puzzling that the present public attitude towards literature is, with some exceptions, of the same kind as that of current scholarship. Whether we are to blame for this one cannot tell, but scholars are probably in some measure to blame. Who knows whether, if scholars were correct in their philosophy, large parts of the general public might not follow them instead of dogmatic theorists and fake specialists in education who now seem to dictate erroneous thinking and the avoidance of literature itself by the use of mere generalities and repetitions? If ordinary people knew that cultural benefit comes only from literature itself, who knows that they would not act on such advice?

Up to this point we have suggested that the total view of humanistic study demands that scholarship should not disregard criticism nor criticism scholarship. The greatest scholars and the greatest critics have rarely, if ever, done so. Indeed, the two go together, and neither is complete without the other. If this is true, there would be a tendency in better minds to break through the barriers into the world of nature, and there are such instances.

An interesting case is that of Sir Philip Sidney,[7] who was a better critic than the doctrine of his age allowed him to be. In *The Defence of Poesy* he adheres firmly to pseudo-Aristotle and censures 'Our tragedies and comedies not without cause cried out against, observing neither honest civility nor skilful poetry.' They violate every one of the three unities, they mix their matter, so that there are 'neither right tragedies nor right comedies', and they 'mingle kings and clowns', thus doing violence to the Horatian principle of decorum. They favour low comedy where there is 'no delight without laughter', which, he says, 'is very wrong'. A short time before, however, he has revealed his weakness, or rather his strength, when he confesses: 'I never heard the old song of Percy and Douglas that I found not my heart moved more than with a trumpet.' But he adds the preposterous suggestion: 'What would it work trimmed in the gorgeous eloquence of Pindar?' He shows his quality as a great critic also in his list of the greatest English poets up to his time: Chaucer, Surrey, Sackville and Spenser, not one of whom was a neo-classicist.

Dryden too was a critic who builded better than he knew.[8] There is no doubt of his commitment to French classical theories, even to his applying them to his own works, and yet in his prefaces, such as that to the *Fables* and that on Satire prefixed to his translation of Persius and Juvenal, he shows an excellence of critical judgement and a naturalness that rival Montaigne. It will be remembered that in the discussions that make up the *Essay of Dramatic Poesy* (1668) it is Dryden who espouses the cause of Shakespeare. In so doing he is guilty of an inconsistency that is still puzzling. If Shakespeare was what Dryden said he was, on what actual bases was he comparable to the poets to whom he is compared? Did Dryden not see with his usual breadth, insight and sympathy what Shakespeare actually was?

He was the man who of all modern, and perhaps ancient poets, had the largest and most comprehensive soul. All the images of Nature were still present to him, and he knew them, not laboriously, but luckily; when he describes anything, you more than see it, you feel it too. Those who acuse him to have wanted learning, give him the greater commendation; he was naturally learned; he needed not the spectacles of books to read Nature: he looked inwards, and found her there.

Dryden, like Sidney, must have had an artificial concept of the relation between nature and art that broke down before his broad knowledge and sympathy and his excellent critical judgement.

The dominance of neo-classicism, with some exceptions that we magnify, continued until the end of the eighteenth century. Then came the Romantic movement, which was to a large extent literary.[9] Kant had opened a new world, and the new point of view was not thought of by its proponents as a mere stylistic revolt. They did not neigh to be shut up in a paddock labelled Romanticism. They thought of the new movement as a dash for liberty, and one should not forget that their rebellion was put down by Victorian formalism and the mixed and inconsequential debate between classicism and romanticism. In the light of the high hopes of August Wilhelm von Schlegel the story has a tragic ending. The passage below is from the translation of John Black: since, however, the original is stronger and clearer, it will be found in the Notes: [10]

We see numbers of men, and even whole nations, so fettered by the conventions of education and habits of life, that, even in the appreciation of the fine arts, they cannot shake them off. Nothing appears to them natural, appropriate, or beautiful, which is alien to their own languages, manners, and social relations. With this exclusive mode of seeing and feeling, it is no doubt possible to attain, by means of cultivation, to a great nicety of discrimination within the narrow circle to which it limits and circumscribes them. But no man can be a true critic or connoisseur without universality of mind, without that flexibility which enables him, by renouncing all personal predilections and blind habits, to adapt himself to the peculiarities of other ages and nations—to feel them, as it were, from their proper central point, and, what ennobles human nature, to recognize and duly appreciate whatever is beautiful and grand under the external accessories which were necessary to its embodying, even though occasionally they may seem to disguise and distort it. There is no monopoly of poetry for particular ages and nations; and consequently that despotism in taste, which would seek to invest with universal authority the rules which at first, perhaps, were but arbitrarily advanced. Poetry, taken in its widest acceptation, as the power of creating what is beautiful, and representing it to the eye or the ear, is a universal gift of Heaven, being shared to a certain extent even by those we call barbarians and savages.

This passage as a whole, other utterances of Schlegel and of other commentators are no mere matters of rebellion against the stylistic and other conventions of neo-classicism but are expressions of a hope for an open world.

So much for the cause of liberty. Present is also the belief that art itself is skill in performance and has the form of a continuum from mere impulsive activity to the highest achievements in the mastery of material. The breakdown of the highest hopes of the Romantic movement does not mean that nothing was accomplished. The range of style and subject was increased, and commerce itself helped to set literature free as a record of human life and its interpretation. But literary critics, always excepting the greatest critics, were not reduced to a small or impotent garrison, but were and are a large, intelligent and active force adhering to the cause of the divine right of literary art.[11]

The situation may be thus described: the concept of literature has, on the whole, been repeatedly broadened from pseudo-Aristotle to the critics and thinkers of our own day. Attempts to make it conform to the infinite breadth of nature have been many. Such attempts have usually met with conservative resistance, but, if they proved their truth by experience, they have, we may believe, usually met with acceptance. Our century has been particularly active in the amplification of the concept—its inclusiveness, origins, motives and its forms. This is as it should be, and the contributions of such writers, mainly philosophers, as Kant, Coleridge, Mill, the symbolists, Croce, Freud, even Marx and Tolstoi, should be examined from the point of view of whether or not they are true. There is no occasion for debate, which merely interferes with the search for truth. The determination is not easy, since it requires thought on high levels of abstraction and demands correctness both as to intension and extension in the logical process. These questions, with a fair exercise of openness of mind will, we may believe, find their answers in the course of time. Meantime, polemics is a waste of effort and a producer of confusion.

If these possible contributions to a more complete comprehension of literature are thought of as such, there need be no great heat engendered, and there might not be were it not that new ideas are often thought of as inimical forces and judged on the narrow ground of whether or not they support or oppose some widely supported current opinion, such as the doctrine of the superhuman origin and nature of works of genius.

Among the warlike moves of defence is one of peculiar effectiveness. It might be described as the practice of labelling. The labels may be impressionistic, socio-realistic, symbolistic, pragmatic, historistic, mechanistic, expressionistic, or any one of a dozen or two other designations thought, wrongly or rightly, to be dominant in an author's thought. He can then be tucked away and discredited. This practice is a complete negation of the belief here held in continuity, gradual accretion of truth, the freedom to think and act, and all-inclusiveness. If a theorist is so silly as to think in this age that the vast problem of art and literature can be solved by a single speculation, he deserves to the extent that he does so to be labelled and pigeon-holed. But this practice of disposing of a scholar or critic as if he were a material object is both unjust and fallacious.

Take the case of Benedetto Croce, who has been labelled 'expressionist'. I do not know exactly what the

label means, but the normal meaning of the word
shocks me when thought of as a fitting adjective to be
applied as a final verdict on a very great scholar, historian and critic. The critics who applied it certainly
did not live, as I did, through days made bright by
Philosophy of the Spirit (1902–17), *Goethe* (1919), and
Ariosto, Shakespeare and Corneille (1920). They could
not have read in the pages of *La Critica* the long series
of articles on almost forgotten poets and prose writers
that gave them back their voices and their membership in the human race.[12] To be sure, Croce in one
of his titles speaks of aesthetics as 'the science of expression', but he equates it with logic as the science of
the pure concept and the philosophy of the practical
concept. To dispose of Benedetto Croce as a mere
'expressionist' (whatever that may mean) is not two
steps this side of the absurd.

Earlier in this book we have suggested that it is an
evidence of the grace of God that even the greatest
and noblest achievement is within the range of human
powers and that there is at this time a new epistemology that would recognize the vastitude of human
environment and set men of every class and condition
free to understand it and operate within it. It has also
been said that along with the new epistemology there
is a theory of cognition that does away with the mystery of genius along with other mysteries and superstitions. A main feature of this theory of cognition is
that it is one operation and not two. The mind seems
to operate as a unit and, so far as we know, without
intermediary action. We may say in mere speculation
that associative connections in the synapses of the
brain are not always predictable but may be routine
or original, customary or new, true or erroneous, but,
in any case, are within the brain. If this is true, it will

be seen at once, that faculty psychology, long ago discredited but still in use, must, if we are to make any progress towards truth, be discontinued as a factor in thought. At the present time these faculties are supernumerary creators and producers of error. Imagination is a fictitious giant, memory a sort of upper servant, reason a mere pensioner and emotion a distrusted hanger-on. The brain is not a household, and cognition is a single operation of which emotion is an integral part.

Literary criticism, by which in this connection I mean literary theory rather than the reading and judging of prose and poetry, has always kept close to philosophy, a thing that of itself seems to recognize the fact that the science that investigates the facts and principles of reality and of human nature and conduct, namely philosophy, applies to literature, even in its most exalted manifestations, as well as to life. I think there is nothing in literature that is not in life, so that this ancient, indeed inevitable, affiliation of life and literature within the bounds of philosophy seems to be both natural and correct, and it is in support of it that the new naturalistic epistemology is adduced.

Literary criticism has tended to follow the philosophical fashion—Aristotle, Horace, Longinus, Quintilian, pseudo-Aristotle, French classicism, Kant, Hegel and Coleridge, and many recent philosophical developments. If literary criticism regards itself as having its own special philosophy, why has it bothered its head with the philosophical attempts to understand and explain mere man and his environment? Literary criticism has been right in seeking light from philosophy, and it is the purpose of this chapter to suggest that more and brighter light can be had in the field

13

of the humanities from the newest and greatest of modern philosophical developments. This philosophy seems to be of quite general application to the fields of fact and truth, and the fact that it has been discovered by physicists should be in its favour.

With this in mind let me suggest that literary criticism needs more philosophy and not less. It also needs to know more about literature, which its theoretical observation tends to make it neglect; that is, more about actuality. Let us pause to remark that in balance and breadth there lies somewhere between the simple and useful descriptions of reviewers and extreme philosophical speculation a body of sound and learned critics. Primarily there is, however, a need of metaphysics, not manufactured to suit preferences and occasions, since the subject is highly developed and well understood. There is a cosmology sufficiently inclusive to embrace the universe—the macrocosm of the heavens and the microcosm of the atom—the whole range of social environment and the habitual and incidental activities of the human race. There is also an ontology that advances far into the nature of being and opens the road to the recognition of actuality, an ontology also that insists that every proposition is true only to the extent that it is based on actuality. Finally, there is an epistemology, as described above, that offers freedom, breadth and inclusiveness.

It is shocking to think that literary criticism should even be willing to think of itself as beyond the limits of God's universe and as governed by special laws incomprehensible to normal human intelligence. That such a creed, which is a sort of rejection of vast inheritance, exists would not be believed were it not met with continually even in unexpected places, indeed if there were not evidence that it is widely held by men of responsibility and intelligence. For example, William K. Wimsatt, Jr., who is principal author of *Literary Criticism: a Short History* (New York, 1957), is a man of learning, good judgement, and moderation. Yet here is what he has finally to say about it:

What is the relation of the poetic or aesthetic emotion to the emotions of real or ordinary life? This difficult question has been implicit in the critical debate from ancient days, with the catharsis of Aristotle or the transport of Longinus, to the recent past, with the incipience and equipoise of Ricardian psychology or the Freudian varieties of worked-off inhibitions. If one has to make a stark choice between the simply realistic theory—that poetry deals with straight emotions of pity, fear, or erotic passion, and that is why we like it—and some theory of artistic modification—that poetry works some change in real-life emotions, and that is why we like it—one must clearly choose the latter.

This answer is guarded and indirect, the style betraying a slight reluctance, but seems to make a clear, and to me disappointing, choice. The difficulty in this case and possibly others may arise from the fact that it deals with emotions from an outgrown point of view. The classification of the emotions in terms of faculty psychology was for centuries futile and unreliable. More than fifty years ago the age-old practice was distrusted and the function of the emotions was seen to be a concomitant of cognition and came to be regarded as a colouring. This was a step in the right direction. The new epistemology regards feeling as an actual part of the cognitive process. It adds to that the idea that emotion is the determining factor in satisfaction, whether of truth or beauty or goodness or what not. When therefore it is seen that emotion is merely an inevitable operative part of all mental activity, the necessity of such decisions as the above vanishes together with its significance.

One must not forget the enormous quantity, the variety and the fertility of the literature of literary criticism in our day. There is no fault to be found with it except in the matter of theories, and here one must except great well-balanced critics whose culture and ability keep them within the bounds of reason. One may, however, believe that in the elapse of time literary criticism will come to a better understanding of itself. The thing to be remembered is that the divorce between scholarship and criticism is unnecessary as well as unfortunate. The process of symbolization demands an integration of art and intellection, so that the one becomes not the mere measure or rival of the other. The symbol and its meaning are aspects of one operation, which, we are told, is the process of mental growth.

CHAPTER IX

RENAISSANCE 1

The alteration of the past is necessary for two
reasons, one of which is subsidiary and, so to speak,
precautionary. The subsidiary reason is that the Party
member, like the proletarian, tolerates present conditions partly because he has no standard of comparison. He must be cut off from the past, just as he must
be cut off from foreign countries, because it is necessary for him to believe that he is better off than his
ancestors and that the average level of material com-
fort is constantly rising. But by far the more important
reason for the readjustment of the past is the need to
safeguard the infallibility of the Party.—George Or-
well, *1984.*

PERHAPS AN idea of the nature of renascence in
general may be gained by a comparison between
the Renaissance of the twelfth century and the
so-called Italian Renaissance. It is absurd to think
that either of them arose from more than a relatively
static cultural situation. It is true that the Middle
Ages, a long period, was marked by unusual continuity of action and custom, but like all periods of
human history it had its full share of changes.

Both periods will be seen to have had their points
of distinguished achievement. For example, the
Twelfth Century Renaissance was marked by the perfection of Romanesque architecture and the beginning
of the Gothic. It had an efflorescence of vernacular
Goliardic verse. It had also a revival of Latin poetry of

high order, and in the Latin drama of the mediaeval church it produced a striking body of Latin literature. Very important also in the period was the amplification and enrichment of the curriculum of learning. From what seems to have been a rather poor form of the trivium (grammar, rhetoric and logic) and the quadrivium (arithmetic, geometry, astronomy—including astrology—and music) the century emerged with the Seven Liberal Arts in greatly improved form and the Three Philosophies (natural, moral and mental) plus Roman and common law, Euclid, Ptolemy, and a great body of Arabic and Greek medicine and philosophy—really a fairly full body of the works of Aristotle as translated and interpreted by the Arabians. Plato the twelfth century did not have except in the restricted form of the earlier Middle Ages. Their culture and their inspiration was Latin and not Greek, and in that respect it differed from the Italian Renaissance. But the earlier renascence had behind it the driving power of a new philosophy. The works of Aristotle furnished the new direction and the proof is in Anselm, Abelard, Gratian, John of Salisbury, and ultimately St. Thomas Aquinas.

In other matters also there were distinct parallels. The twelfth century was prosperous, a prosperity abundantly shared by the church. It shows itself in a great increase in travel and communication, in an increase in urban life and in a great increase in the collecting and copying of books. This growth in wealth, as well as this quickening of the spirit, appears in possibly the greatest social achievement of the twelfth century, namely, the development of cathedral and monastic schools into universities. Philip Augustus granted a charter to the University of Paris in the year 1200. No fact could better witness the breadth of the twelfth-century Reinaissance than the institution of universities. Like the Italian Renaissance, it was a great age of transition.

There were also a surprising number of centres of intellectual culture: Toledo, St. Gall, Bec, Bologna, Laon, Liege, Paris and a large number of other places. What we have are pilgrimages, romances sung by minstrels, schools engaged in disputation, courts, castles, great cathedrals, and better roads. One must not forget the literary renascence in Provence that did so much to awaken the genius of Dante.[1]

There is thus a close resemblance between the two most clearly marked re-awakenings in modern history. This seems to tell us clearly that neither of them was solely a renascence of art and letters. Because of other connections and their proximity in time one might also infer that the chain of revivals in various countries of Europe are properly thought of as successive manifestations of the same great impulse, although of course Spain, France, the Rhine valley and England had each its different beginning, growth and character. There is thus a sense in which they may be regarded as separate movements.

More generally also it would perhaps be agreed that, although the Italian Renaissance was far greater and more important than any other, being as it was the awakening of the world, the history of the arts, sciences and general learning, as also of commerce, manufacture, and the science and art of government, records many awakenings, great and small. Religion seems to be full of them. What these re-awakenings were, what inter-relations they had seems not to be known. Re-awakenings seem also to be regional or actually local, since it is obvious that often a very small group of persons have done outstanding things. It therefore seems worth while to enquire into the possibility of a renascence in the modern world, a great one if possible, although a little one would be better than patterned stagnation. Also, although there is little hope of finding an answer, one would like to know why renascences come to an end. The current belief that society is inevitably rhythmical in its advances and retrogressions does not accord well with a whole world infinitely varied in its philosophies, trends, conditions and motives.

Consider the English Renaissance of the sixteenth century. One would like to know whether it is necessary to be mystical. In that small, ill-developed kingdom of England with about as many inhabitants alltold as there are in Chicago there appeared an intellectual and artistic greatness that is sufficiently witnessed by such names as Sir Thomas More and Roger Ascham, Sir Philip Sidney and Edmund Spenser, Richard Hooker and Sir Francis Bacon, Christopher Marlowe and William Shakespeare, William Gilbert and William Harvey, with some hundreds of other notable names. Setting aside all modern advantages, if any country in the world, however large, wealthy and important, could in proportion to population, produce such a percentage of greatness, it would be then and there the greatest nation in the world.

But it might be said that everything has been done, and this, within the limitations laid down for discursive subjects by superstition, authority and the philosophy of the scientific method applied to discursive subjects, would in some measure be true. It is, however, an ignorant idea. If we had a philosophy of breadth and freedom, one applicable to discursive fields, no one knows what the future of religion, philosophy, the social sciences and the humanities might be. We know only that there is a vast unknown and unimaginable area as yet unexplored. We should have only a naturally adapted method and the freedom to follow it. And we should have a new direction.

Among the many factors which have been recognized as effective in the creation and growth of the Renaissance the one chosen for emphasis here is the promise of unbelievably good things held out to those who acquired learning. From this point of view the Renaissance in England came, in some measure, as the result of propaganda. Perhaps there is no reason to doubt that the Renaissance in western Europe in all its principal centres, Italy, France, Spain, the Low Countries, and England, arose out of practically the same conditions and assumed in various centres characteristic local or national differences.

John Addington Symonds and other scholars have stressed the relative importance of the classical revival, but even in Symonds there is no disposition to make light of other factors. 'It was scholarship,' he says, 'first and last, which revealed to men the wealth of their own minds.'[2] 'Contact with Islam in the south and east, diplomatic relations with the Turks, familiarity with the mixed races of Spain, and commerce with the nations of the north had widened the sympathies of the Italians, and taught them to regard humanity as one large family.'[3] Although he gives the Revival of Learning as the first cause of the Renaissance, he mentions the following considerations as the second cause: 'Instead of empire and papacy, the sun and moon of the medieval system, a federation of peoples, separate in type and divergent in interests, yet bound together by common tendencies, common culture and common efforts, came into existence.'[4] Symonds also allows for the force of reaction against the dominant ideas of the Middle Ages, then becoming obsolete. The late R. C. Jebb in the *Cambridge Modern History*[5] dwells particularly on the Revival of Learning in two aspects: 'the recovery of a lost culture and the renewed diffusion of a liberal spirit which for centuries had been dead or sleeping'. There is no doubt that the Renaissance in England owed much to the actual and immediate influence of the classics in the sense in which Symonds and Jebb understood it.[6] Miss Edith Sichel sees the Renaissance as 'the result of a universal impulse, and that impulse was preceded by something like a revelation, a revelation of intellect and of the possibilities of men'.[7]

Burckhardt, as is well known, takes a much less mystical view. He stresses the development of cities and the equality of classes.

We must insist upon it, as one of the chief propositions of this book, that it was not the revival of antiquity alone, but its union with the genius of the Italian people, which achieved the conquest of the western world. . . . But the great and general enthusiasm of the Italians for classical antiquity did not display itself before the fourteenth century. For this a development of civic life was required, which took place only in Italy, and there not till then. It was needful that noble and burger should first learn to dwell together on equal terms, and that a social world should arise which felt the want of culture and had the leisure and means to obtain it.[8]

Almost no historian of the Renaissance fails to call attention to the importance of the printing press as a means of stimulating, through a more general education, the activities of the Renaissance.[9]

The Renaissance in England was obviously moral, political, and religious, like the Renaissance in the Low Countries; but it was also intensely ambitious and practical. The latter quality appears also strongly in Italy and France. When any issue presented itself, the Englishman of the sixteenth century tended to choose that aspect of it which had most to offer. To realize this commonplace one has only to consider Francis Bacon and his ambition to carry to completion man's domination over nature. There was on the one side an element of faith and on the other an element of promise. What the eighteenth century and the nineteenth century had to offer as the reward of learning was as nothing to what the sixteenth century professed itself able to do. The science or pseudo-science of the English Renaissance was ready to explain everything. Its claims were infinite. It could cure man's body, save his soul, provide him with foreknowledge, develop his power of mind, make his fortune in money or love, arm him against passion in himself or deceit in others, and allocate him not only in the material but in the spiritual world. In order that man might avail himself of these opportunities it was necessary that he should be free and should know how to read. The invention of printing and the cheapness of printed books had made provision for the latter, and the former was provided for in the freedom of the will with which he was endowed by his theology and psychology. He had before him both the necessity and the opportunity of seeking his own salvation.

What happened in the English Renaissance was not supersession of old ideas by new. It is doubtful if that has ever so happened or could happen. It was rather a development of the implications which learning, classical and scholastic, had always had. The mediaeval world had had a large share of the doctrines of antiquity, and an extensive body of dicta, well organized by St. Thomas Aquinas and the Schoolmen, for the explanation and co-ordination of the visible universe and the solution of the problems of living the human life. The new learning was mainly engaged in showing the possibilities of the old. There was nothing destructive of foundation until the time of Bacon and Hobbes. Not only had the seven liberal arts been greatly amplified and improved after the reintroduction into Europe of the writings of Aristotle and other ancients, but in the thirteenth century there had been added to the curriculum the three philosophies. The effect of the introduction of the three philosophies into the curriculum was to create the widespread knowledge of cosmology and psychology which is found among learned men in the fourteenth, fifteenth and sixteenth centuries.[10]

We are familiar with the Renaissance belief in a perfectly organized universe, every part of which had its place, its functions, and its inter-relations. There were the microcosm with its intricate correspondences with the macrocosm, the hierarchy of the angels and the theory of disembodied or original spirits, the correspondences between both and the universe, the doctrine of spirits, humours, and temperaments, and the vast belief in analogies and types according to which everything on earth had its significance and every evil its antidote, the whole constituting a grand machine through which Providence or fate operated.[11] The Renaissance assisted men to believe all this, to believe in a world immediately under God's guidance and having about it possibilities of perfection and achievement ready to yield to virtue and reason, which were one and the same. Common men had never before known the possibilities of this world as plainly revealed by science and philosophy and had never before had a chance to exploit them. One can understand the bright zeal of the men of the Renaissance when they learned of this bonanza.

In reviewing what the various sciences had to offer let us begin with the ancient science of logic. Throughout all the activities of the Romans and the Schoolmen the logic of Aristotle had remained unchanged. It carried with it, and still carries with it, a flattering promise of power. Even the changes of Ramus are not essential. He merely inverted the traditional order and treated *invention* before *judgement*. What he does is to announce a practical end and declare (with Faustus), *Bene dissere est finis logices.* Logic as he expounds it is not only an instrument for the ascertainment of truth and the detection of error, but also a means of interpreting the word of God, a veritable key to the mind of God.[12] The claims of the followers of Ramus are also most extensive. Dudley Fenner, *The Artes of Logike and Rethorike* (1584) offers a method of government in the family, the upbringing of children, and the clarification of the Scriptures. Abraham Fraunce, *Lawiers Logike* (1588 and two other issues) though drawing his examples from Spenser and the poets, claims to set to rights the analysis of legal causes. The logic of Aristotle in the form given it by Melancthon held sway over the Protestant world; but even Thomas Blundeville (*The Art of Logic*, 1599, 1611, 1619) and Thomas Wilson (*The Rule of Reason*, 1551, 1552, 1553, 1567, 1584?, 1593), both of whom are Aristotelians, are not behind the Ramists in their claims. Logic to them was a study by means of which a Protestant man might find out the truth, elude the devil and his agents, and thus achieve salvation.

The claims of ethics were stupendous. It told men how to be successful as well as how to be good, and was popular for that reason. These claims are to be found in Boethius and throughout the Middle Ages, but it required the re-introduction of Aristotelian ethics, as interpreted by the Italians, to make the subject sufficiently enticing. There were two methods of ethical study side by side in the latter half of the sixteenth century. There were the books of the Sayings of the Wise, to which the *Dictes and Sayings of Philosophers* occupied a somewhat original position. Such books continued to be made and remade, printed and reprinted, throughout the sixteenth century and most of the next. The great vogue and long continuance of these sayings of the wise seems to indicate stirrings of aspiration in relatively unlearned levels of the Renaissance population who were trying to master bits of eternal truth, or what they thought were such.[13] About the middle of the century the *Ethics* of Aristotle appeared and no doubt became more popularly known.[14] Aristotelian ethics was not, however, read so much in its original form as in adaptations. There was a flood of Italian and French ethical works increasing as the sixteenth century went on. It is these that interpret the possibilities of ethical study. The sixteenth century placed before itself the ideal of developing the different faculties of man, the ideal of universality, and there was nothing in their psychology which precluded achievement on equal terms by every human soul, since the soul, as a divine substance, was illimitable and needed only to realize itself through the flesh.

Perhaps the subject that concerned ethical thinkers most was the qualities and functions of the perfect prince and the perfect courtier, a subject still uppermost in the mind of Francis Bacon, as witnessed by his *Advice to Sir George Villiers Afterwards Duke of Buckingham* and many other writings. The sixteenth century treated the subject of the perfect prince with a meticulousness of detail rarely equalled in the world's literature.[15]

An indication that the learning of the age sifted down to the plain people from the classes ordinarily called educated is furnished by a quite marvellous book of morals for ordinary citizens, the title-page of which indicates its scope: *The Court of Good Counsel. Wherein is set down the true Rules, how a man should choose a good Wife from a bad. Wherein is also expressed the great care that Parents should have, for the Bestowing of their Children in Marriage: And likewise how Children ought to behave themselves towards their Parents: And howe Maisters ought to governe their Servants, and how Servants ought to be obedient towards their Maisters,* 1607.

The literature of politics is of course closely related to the literature of ethics, particularly to that part of ethics that had to do with the perfect prince and courtier. But the subject of politics in general held out promises of well-being in peace and war which no nation, having faith, would willingly disregard. The prevailing interest was moralistic and practical. Of the books on the courtier that made their way into England, or were written in England, emphasis is laid on those that present the statesman rather than the man of manners. Castiglione's *Il Cortegiano* was far more influential in England than was Della Casa's *Galateo*, the other most popular Italian book of the type. The difference of emphasis of these two books, the latter on the courtly character proper, the former on the statesman and man of affairs, is the one to which I wish to call attention. Hoby's translation of the *Courtier* was published in 1561, 1577, 1588, and 1603. R. Peterson's translation of *Galateo* was published but once, 1576. English courtly writings usually resemble *The Courtier* rather than *Galateo*; as, for example, Sir Thomas Elyot's *The Governour*, which was printed eight times in the sixteenth century (1531, 1537, 1544, 1546, 1553, 1565, 1580). There were many other books of the same trend, such as Sir William Segar's *The Booke of Honor and Armes*, 1590, and *Honor, Military and Civill*, 1602; and the anonymous *The Institution of a Gentleman*, 1555, 1568.

Polydore Vergil certainly did much to establish the governmental tradition of the Tudors. He had definite ideas of the function of the historiographer and so shaped and pointed the events of the reigns preceding that of Henry VII that he was followed in his conception of the nature of kingship and the validity of the Tudor right by Hall, Fox, Burnet, Strype, Holinshed, and the authors of *A Mirror for Magistrates,* as well as by Daniel, Drayton, Warner, and the main body of the historical dramatists. Thomas Cromwell and the men he influenced were avowed students of Machiavelli, whose influence, on its serious and unprejudiced side, continued down to Bacon himself. Croft's edition of *The Governour* and subsequent discoveries with reference to sources reveal Sir Thomas Elyot's familiarity with a great body of mainly Italian literature on the royal theme. John Ponet, Bishop of Worcester, published (possibly at Strassburg) *A Short Treatise of Polityke Power* in 1556, which was of enough importance to be again reprinted in London in 1639. William Thomas's *The Historie of Italie* is a political document and went through at least two editions (1549, 1561). Thomas Bedingfield's preface to his translation of *The Florentine Historie*, 1595, shows his serious political purpose. Lewis Einstein calls attention to the political ideas which underlay John

Leslie's *A Defense of the Honour of Marie Queene of Scotlande* (1569, 1571, 1584) and Charles Merbury's *A Briefe Discourse of Royall Monarchie*, 1581.[16] The breadth, fairness and learning of that shrewd and plausible book attributed to Parsons the Jesuit has not been fully recognized. It is entitled *A Conference about the Next Succession to the Crowne of England*, is dedicated to the Earl of Essex and was published in 1594.

In the wider field of political thinking who can estimate the influence of Guevara? The sixteenth century knew no more popular books than *The Golden Boke of Marcus Aurelius* translated by Lord Berners (1535, 1537, 1539, 1542, 1546, 1553, 1557 bis, 1573, 1586) and *The Diall of Princes* translated by Thomas North (1557, 1568, 1582, 1586). There were of course many books on manners, some of them well known, but it has seemed to me that serious treatises on civil life were more numerous and more widely read. Guicciardini, for example, had a great vogue in England. *The Historie of Guicciardini, conteining the Warres of Italy,* was translated by Geoffrey Fenton and published twice in the year 1579, in 1594, and again in 1618. *A Briefe Collection of all the Notable Things in the Hystorie of Guicciarcine* was published in 1595. Nannini's *Civill Considerations upon many and sundrie Histories* (from the French of Chappuys in 1601) is based 'principallie upon those of Guicciardini'. There was also *The Two Discourses of Master F. Guicciardin* (1595), supposed to contain anti-papistical matters suppressed in the Italian editions. One of the really important political treatises of the time was written by an Englishman, Sir Thomas Smith, whose *De Republica Anglorum* had been published ten times by 1640 (1583, 1584, 1589, 1594, 1601, 1607, 1612, 1621,

14

1625, 1640). Jean Bodin's *The Six Books of a Commonweale*, a book of wide scope and perfect Renaissance political point of view, was translated by Richard Knolles and published sumptuously in 1606. One might also mention the widely circulated writings of King James I or dwell on the influence of More's *Utopia*, a book of everlasting significance.

The political element in pure literature is also striking. The political as well as the moral significance of the *Faerie Queene* has long been recognized. The same thing is of course true of the historical plays of Shakespeare. Indeed, taking the Elizabethan drama as a whole, it may be said that in its serious aspect it deals preferably with kings, princes, courts, and courtiers.[17]

Nothing need be said about the claims of alchemy, but one would like to cite an illustration of the respect in which the science of prognostication was held by scholarly men. Robert Record's *Castell of Knowledge* was published in 1556. The preface indicated the solid ground on which judicial astronomy stood. It declares that man is given eyes in order that he may see the heavens and know the importance of his earthly life. God wills that nothing shall happen on earth without warning. There is no great change in the world— alteration of empire, dearth, penury, scarcely the fall of princes—of which God does not premonish man by signs in the heavens. This is too well known to need illustration. Many men besides Noah might have seen the signs of the approaching Flood. Record cites portents in the cases of Ptolemy and Manlius and at the founding and fall of Rome. The commander of the Athenian expedition against Syracuse blindfolded his eyes so that he might disregard the portent of the eclipse of the sun as his expedition was setting out on its disastrous voyage. All these examples show how necessary it is to observe the heavens; since, however, he is not a judicial astronomer, he will devote himself to the explanation of the sphere and thus render the calculations of those who interpret God's will more accurate. He then proceeds to write a sound treatise on astronomy, which he closes with several excellent demonstrations of the rotundity of the earth.

My typical example of the claims of Renaissance learning may be drawn from the field of Elizabethan psychology. The psychology of Aristotle and the Greeks had, by the time of the Renaissance, been organized into consistent treatises, such as those of Arnold of Villa Nova, Constantinus Africanus, Gilbertus Anglicus, Hugo of St. Victor, Isador of Seville, Nemesius, Bartholomaeus,[18] and Francisco Suarez. To these should be added Vives' *De Anima et Vita* and Melancthon's *De Anima*. These treatises, or rather these various versions of one treatise, indicate the state of knowledge throughout most of the sixteenth century. The subject was closely connected with medicine, so that a book like Elyot's *Castell of Helthe* (published at least fourteen times in the sixteenth century) presents just such a system as Galen had developed from Hippocrates. Towards the end of the century the implications of psychology as regards character and sanity as well as health began to be more and more recognized, and stress began to be laid on the pathological aspects of psychology. The earliest of these specialized treatises in English is the famous *A Treatise of Melancholy* by Dr. Timothy Bright (1586 bis, 1613). An idea of the European development of the subject can be gained from the numerous references in Burton's *Anatomy of Melancholy*.[19] Meantime, Luis Vives in *De Anima et Vita* and in his educational writings had

developed the doctrine of the passions of the mind as
they function in education and in life. This lead was
followed by Huarte Navarro, a translation of whose
Examen de Ingenios, the Examination of Men's Wits
was entered in the Stationers' Register in 1590 and
published in 1594. It was extremely popular in England, there being three issues in 1594, others in 1596,
1604, 1616. It shows the specialization of the science
already far advanced. There is nothing comparable to
the claims which it put forward, except only the intelligence testing of our own day. Huarte will show
by discovering the variety of natures in man the profession for which each human being is fitted. By observing and testing the mixture of the four humours
in each man it can be told for what occupation he is
apt. From hot, cold, moist and dry come all differences
of wit. Men of great wisdom and knowledge should be
deputed by the state to discover each one's constitution
at a tender age and cause him perforce to study that
science which is agreeable to his adviser and not permit him to make his own choice. The book provides
signs and tests by which every temperament may be
known and is as scientific and authoritative in tone
and language as any treatise, even psychological, of
our day.

The consideration of the passions as they manifest
themselves in ordinary life and conduct, not primarily
either applied psychology or abnormal psychology, became very general. Spenser has a study of the passions
in the second book of the *Faerie Queene*. There are
also Fletcher's *Purple Island*, Sir John Davies' *Nosce
Teipsum*, and many others. Minor writings, both
scientific and popular, became extremely numerous,
and the psychology of the passions enters into the treatment of many subjects. In 1601 appeared Thomas

Wright's *The Passions of the Minde in Generall* and Charron's *De la Sagesse* (translated by Samson Lennard and entered in the Stationers' Register in July 1606; other editions about 1612, 1640, and later). Wright was re-issued in 1604, 1620, 1621, 1630; and Charron may be said to have been one of the most popular manuals of the seventeenth century. Both books exploit scientifically the nature and action of the passions of the mind. They have the highest possible sanction and may be said (with others) to mark the discovery of the passions, a new force to be controlled and capable of control. Man had known of his passions ever since he had known anything about himself; here was the discovery that they were a group of devil-allied tendencies that might drive him to crime, madness, or the loss of his immortal soul.

Writers like Marlowe, Shakespeare, and Chapman, and now and then Jonson, not only use psychological terms but explain psychological processes. Shakespeare shows himself conscious of the physical concomitants of emotion in his depiction of the jealousy of Othello, the anger of Hotspur, the pride of Coriolanus, the terror of Macbeth, the melancholy of Hamlet, the lust of Angelo, and the envy of Iago. The comedy of humours in Elizabethan drama is an application of the psychology of temperament. The absorbing interest in human passion which appears in Beaumont and Fletcher and the Jacobean dramatists, though expressed in a less crudely technical manner, is but a continuation of the earlier interest in psychology. By and large, Aristotelian psychology, however mistaken in its physiology and anatomy, is a good working basis for the consideration of what goes on in the emotional life of man, and it is obvious that the knowledge of this subject added much to the confidence with which the English Renaissance exploited the life of feelings and emotion.

There appeared also in England a version of the widely known treatise on memory, the claims of which are typical: *The Castel of Memorie: wherein is conteyned the restoryng, augmentyng, and conservyng of the Memorye and Remembraunce; wyth the safest remedyes, and best precepts thereunto in any wyse apperteyning.* By Gulielmus Gratarolus and translated by W. Fulwod, 1562, 1563, 1573. It not only presents the traditional discursus on mnemonics, but it presents the medical aspect of the subject and the dietary aspect. The author advises against the eating of fuming meats, sleeping with one's shoes on, and licentiousness as bad for the memory. He thinks that chewing mastic to purge the head, washing the head and feet, and taking exercise are good for the memory. He gives prescription of medicines for bad memory. The system of memory training outlined goes back originally to Aristotle and is sound enough, but it is accompanied by mnemonic devices and various superstitions and absurdities which are obviously intended as a road to success. The book not only commends goodness of memory, but puts down practical rules by means of which the reader may secure that blessing.

So it is throughout; everywhere is promise of unbelievably good things to those who follow the directions of the learned. This state of the case no doubt reflects the hopefulness of the age. May it not in some measure have created that hopefulness? When all due allowance has been made for title-pages intended to advertise the book and claims stated for the purpose of making the book sell, the fact remains that the literature of learning in the English Renaissance promised power and achievement and proceeded on the basis of the perfectability of man. The theories advanced to explain the genesis of the Renaissance have already been briefly mentioned. The modest contention of this chapter, a contention that will no doubt be readily granted, is that the Renaissance in England came, not altogether because of the influence of the art of antiquity and of Italy, not altogether because men grew rich and comfortable in the prosperity of English commerce during a long period of peace, not altogether because social castes broke down and gave men in the lower ranks a chance to climb to higher stations, but also, in some measure, because men were offered a series of magnificent promises and were foolish enough, or wise enough, to believe them. Out of their faith came their effort, and out of their effort came the awakening of their spirits.

The preceding attempt to enumerate and assess the factors of renascence as they appeared in the twelfth and the sixteenth century is certainly true, although it may be vague. When we try, however, to locate parallel forces and situations in our own time in our own culture, the difficulties increase and the harvest is small.

Discursive subjects, not the sciences, are not static so much as narrow and formalized, although in the interest they arouse there are features of indifference and disregard that are certainly static. In that respect it may be said that we resemble the earlier if not the later Renaissance, but this only repeats the idea that we are in need of an awakening. It may also be said that we have before us a new philosophy if we choose to master it and adopt it, and this, as we shall see, is an important matter. On the other hand, we compare very badly with the Renaissance in desire for learning and culture and in belief that learning and culture have anything desirable to offer. The profession of learning commands little respect and is at best of mediocre standing. Indeed, the post-war years with engrossment in commerce, moving from place to place and mere amusement have manifested a good deal of actual anti-intellectualism.

Because it has a practical bearing on renascence in general, something more hopeful appears in the fact of centres of culture, a feature of both the twelfth century and the later Renaissance. It does not take large numbers of people to bring about a renascence. Some association of persons of like interests is certainly necessary, but groups may be of almost any size. One would even suggest that this may be the way in which renascences begin and grow, that is, by the increase of numbers not of individuals but of groups. The idea of the awakening of a nation seems, as an undertaking, to be nonsense. But the effect of this theory, if it has any validity, would suggest possibilities of promotion. If, for example, certain colleges and universities in our country did what they are supposed to do anyhow— if any of them or some of them promoted actual interest and proficiency in a modern equivalent of the seven liberal arts and the three philosophies to the comparative disregard of merely utilitarian or what may be thought of as 'practical' subjects, these institutions, scattered here and there, might become cultural centres in a very real sense. I am firmly convinced moreover that they would find it profitable and find a new and deep satisfaction in it.

The quotation from John Addington Symonds above has also a practical aspect. He actually says that Renaissance scholarship 'revealed to men the wealth of their own minds'. This was years and years before there appeared the physiological theory as to the

neural basis of almost unlimited mental powers mentioned above. I lower the dignity of this paragraph
when I say that this idea will 'sell' since most men
and women in the academic world are very willing to
believe that they are geniuses. My idea would be to
let them try.

In the liberal spirit in humanistic scholarship we
rank low, but possibly with less excuse, no lower than
scholars in the ages of religious and political persecu-
tion. Ours is possibly a purer kind of dogmatism than
was theirs. As to our promises, we offer very little compared to the Renaissance. It is the advertising world
that offers the panaceas, possibly quite as ineffectual
as the list given above. I respect this, for I know, as
some of my colleagues do, that there is no royal road
to Greek or to cultural excellence. Political interest
is on the wane, and no wonder, since our government
has grown far away and very expensive. As to facilities
—books, journals, comforts and trained assistance—we
surpass the Renaissance fifty or one hundred to one.
But we have found out at last that opportunities to
work do not bring with them zeal. The modern man
seems to resemble the coloured farm-labourer of my
boyhood who assured me that he was not afraid of
work, in fact could lie right down in the cornfield and
sleep in the presence of it.

Comparison of our age with the two selected towering emergences of brains and spirit in our history yields
no convincing pattern of renascence, and, when we
look at the matter negatively, the prospects do not
grow brighter. We have, in such efforts as we have
made in our country to raise the cultural level of our
fellow citizens, perhaps been mistaken as to the things
we thought adequate or essential to success. We
thought we might succeed if we could diminish ignor-

ance, poverty and disease and at the same time provide opportunity, but it may be that hardships themselves have certain spiritual values. What we have done in the modern world in the amelioration of the conditions of life and the betterment of social justice were well meant and desirable, but we have not found the answer. Perhaps we have made two mistakes. We have made these comforts an end in themselves and still have no idea except more comforts, more wealth and more amusement. Secondly—I am almost afraid to say this—it seems that selfishness and sin accompany the rise in the standard of living. Whether that is true or not, we are forced to believe that renascences are matters of spirit and not of matter. It may be that they rest on faith in the eternal ideas of the right in its widest sense. I mean the eternal ideas that have somehow operated on human beings for their betterment from the beginning. If so, these will go on, and what we are writing about is the possibility of acceleration.

The Twelfth Century Renaissance and the Italian Renaissance seem to have had propulsions we do not understand. They were certainly more religious and with all their violence were probably, to use their word, 'gentler' than we are. To them the Seven Bedesmen were real and did not exercise their duties merely by writing cheques. The entertainment of the stranger, the feeding of the hungry, the clothing of the naked, the caring for poor prisoners, the comforting of the dying, the burial of the dead and the caring for widows and orphans are no doubt more efficiently done in our times, but benefactors themselves get less out of their benefactions. Without assurance of human possibilities such as we have, they acted on faith and succeeded because they thought they could.

But one need not be tedious about these things, since

nobody, whether he is writing a book or not, knows much about it. To be sure, we lack the continuity and persistence of the Middle Ages and the open-eyed objective energy of the Renaissance, but who knows whether we might not learn these things?

CHAPTER X

RENAISSANCE 2

I cannot but be raised in this persuasion, that this
third period of time will far surpass that of the Grecian
and Roman learning; only if men will know their own
strength and their own weakness both; and take one
from the other light of invention, and not fire of
contradiction; and esteem of the inquisition of truth
as of an enterprise, and not as of a quality or ornament; and employ wit and magnificence of things of
worth and excellency, and not to things vulgar and of
popular estimation.—Bacon, *Advancement of Learning.*

THE PRECEDING description of the present
state of the study of the humanities, particularly
of English language and literature, might be
considered tentatively from three points of view: its
intellectual or scholastic aspect, its social and personal
aspect, and its spirit treated mainly from the point of
view of actual participation as opposed to the attitude
of mere spectatorship and the practice of avoidance.
The object is not only to assure the survival of one of
the great stays and supports of our civilization, but
partly by ridding it of its obstructions, also to bring
about its improvement and the growth of its power.
These matters have been touched upon in the preceding chapters and some of them treated at consider-
able length. They are presented as subjects for
thought and reflection, and an endeavour has been
made to avoid dogmatism. Indeed, it is not denied that
we are doing tolerably well in spite of very serious

difficulties arising in part from the age in which we live, from a none-too-good inheritance and from a cramped position in the academic world. We must devote this chapter to the puzzling, if not precarious, attempt to assess future prospects.

Actually we have been over-departmentalized and made into a specialty. This might in part be justified as a matter of practical operation, but it has, as said above, robbed us of our central position in the intellectual life, that is, in the function we might exercise in symbolization, since we profess the language and literature of our own race and country. This is of course discharged to some degree by those engaged in other fields, but it is originally in our territory. Those who work in other fields than ours have as much need for the correct fitting of words to entities as we have, and it may be that we could, if we knew more, be more useful than we have been. It does not help our case to remember that we consented willingly to being treated as a mere specialty. We possibly failed to see the importance of our position in general education. Did we not know that Latin, almost universally studied, filled this general educational need? We are those who might have taught the orderly fitting of symbols to objects and events. In the course of narrowing that we have accepted without protest, it is perhaps true that we have not known enough, because of our close specialization, to serve the needs of those who study other subjects than ours. This was quite unnecessary, since the human mind is practically without limits, and time is the only condition. Nor is there any limit to what a scholar in our field needs to know.

These statements sound like charges, but they are not so. The matter is relative and perfection is inevitably a matter of degree. Almost anybody with experience in organization knows that, in order to achieve proper functioning, it is necessary to adjust to regulations and current faults and to achieve one's ends in spite of them. Thus it has not been and will not be said that any adverse criticisms here made apply to the whole practice of humanistic studies, much less to all persons engaged in them. This is merely an attempt to frame an ideal or pattern of action, which asks for knowledge and judgement, not debate.

All recorded cases of intellectual advance by races and groups have had behind them some new philosophy that has endeavoured to combat or correct an established method or way of looking at life and its problems and issues. We have at this time, as explained above, what looks like a great philosophical advance in the mastery and methodology of our subject. It is argued above that this new philosophy, particularly its epistemology, has particular application to discursive subjects, and to our special subject because it promises us a freedom of which we are greatly in need. This makes it necessary to explain what is meant by this and point out the ways in which the current method of seeking truth seems to be in error or merely unproductive. It does not of course discredit or seek to replace the older way of working and understanding except in certain matters. It ought not to be necessary in the modern world to explain Karl Pearson's idea of the incremental growth of the knowledge of truth.[1] It would be absurd to assert that the philosophy of relativity supersedes the philosophy behind the scientific method, but it is not absurd to say that it seeks to correct it, amplifies it and seeks to make the total philosophy of learning more adequate and more in line with nature; it also limits the area of the operation of positivism. Specifically it seems to say that, if we could rid ourselves of various obstructions and impediments, we might see before us a region unknown but certainly important, a possibility of progress that might mean much to human culture.

This book finds no fault with the great works done and being done by scholars in our field, but it does say that it is not nuclear physics only that our world needs. It needs also a better *modus vivendi*, a better ethics, politics and economics and a greater respect for law and order. It needs to revive its knowledge of Plato's great discovery of twenty-three hundred years ago of the difference between things that are permanent and things that are merely transitory. It needs to rise to an intellectual level on which that discovery itself may be developed and applied. It also asks what we mean to do with the vast and meticulously tested assemblage of materials we have collected for investigation. Do we mean to use it without studying it as a basis of unsupported speculation or are we going to read it and find out what it may mean? This is no time for avoidance, but for effort and understanding. The corpus is very large, and it may be that we could save time by neglecting or discarding great masses of mere opinion and by devoting ourselves mainly to actual works and original records and to thinking about them. The truth does not often appear in mere consensus of casual opinion or from debate.

The preceding chapter gives a summary account of certain revivals of learning and culture that belong to our background and suggests that there have been many such revivals great and small; in fact, that renascences are a social habit. It thinks so well of them that it expresses the belief that we in the discursive fields of learning are in need of one just now. Just as a matter of possibly wishful thinking may we be indulged in offering a no doubt highly speculative and dubious discussion of a renascence now? We have expressed our belief that in the various discursive fields there are great discoveries and achievements as yet to be made. We have even gone so far as to express the opinion that, if our methods of approach were more effective and if we had faith, which in one sense is the courage to hope and labour to a larger end, we might take our place with the natural sciences in the advancement of learning.

The subject of human progress is both vast and vague and each individual can only do his tiny part, but it has been the subject of much discussion.[2] This is of course not the place to record even the barest of outlines, but it might lend some interest to cite some actual cases.

One April day some years ago I encountered in my reading two paragraphs by two eminent men. The first was by Sir Winston Churchill and formed a part of his address before the Massachusetts Institute of Technology:[3]

But the soul of man thus held in trance or frozen in a long night can be awakened by a spark coming from God knows where, and in a moment the whole structure of lies and oppression is on trial for its life. Peoples in bondage should never despair. Science no doubt could, if sufficiently perverted, exterminate us all; but it is not in the power of material forces in any period which the youngest here tonight need take into practical account, to alter the main element in human nature or restrict the infinite variety of forms in which the souls and genius of the human race will express itself.

Sir Winston does not often indulge in philosophic speculations, and yet nobody doubts that he is capable of philosophical thinking. Note that he says 'can be awakened' and that the kindling is to be done by 'a spark coming from God knows where'. It is plainly a case for the consultation of Arnold J. Toynbee, who tells us that, when hardships and difficulties are met and overcome and neither dodged and avoided nor merely endured, man progresses and grows great in a fuller realization of his possibilities. The difference between him and Sir Winston Churchill, if there is a difference, seems to be that Sir Winston thinks that rescue or revival is inevitable and Toynbee does not. The following from *A Study of History*[4] will illustrate a point of probable agreement between the two:

> It was not without cause that Bunyan's Christian was so greatly distressed.
> 'I am for certain informed (said he) that this our city will be burned with fire from Heaven—in which fearful overthrow both myself and thee my wife and you my sweet babes shall miserably come to ruine, except (the which I see not) some way of escape can be found, whereby we may be delivered.'
> What response to this challenge is Christian going to make? Is he going to look this way and that as if he were going to run—and run on crying 'Life! Life! Eternal life!—with his eye set on a shining light and his feet bound for a distant wicket-gate? If the answer to this question depended on nobody but Christian himself, our knowledge of the uniformity of human nature might incline us to predict that Christian's imminent destiny was Death in his City of Destruction. But in the classic version of the myth we are told that the human protagonist was not left entirely to his own resources in the decisive hour. According to John Bunyan, Christian was saved by his encounter with Evangelist. And, in as much as it cannot be supposed that God's nature is less constant than Man's, we may and must pray that a reprieve which God has granted our society once will not be refused if we ask for it again in a humble spirit and with a contrite heart.

Sir Winston Churchill seems to rely on a kindling spark and Mr. Toynbee on Evangelist; but, in either

case, we may accept as a working basis the principle
of progress through the conquest of difficulty in a situation in which we hope to pass, not from slavery to
freedom, but from mediocrity to excellence. In case
it should be thought that we compare small things
with great, let it be denied. To be sure, the City of
Destruction is afraid of fire, but it is the spark from
heaven that it dreads. We have made provision for
getting along without it. We remove from the paths of
our students those difficulties that Toynbee tells us
must be surmounted if progress is to be made. Sir
Winston said, 'People in bondage should never
despair,' and I say, 'Universities in bondage (to commonplace materialism) and bound hand and foot by
complacent dogmatism should never despair.'

The following paragraph from Alfred North Whitehead's *Science and the Modern World*[5] has some
bearing:

There is another side to this picture of the possibility
of decadence. At the present moment a discussion is
raging as to the future of civilization in the novel circumstances of rapid scientific and technological advance. The
evils of the future have been diagnosed in various ways,
the loss of religious faith, the malignant use of material
power, the degradation attending a differential birth-
rate favouring the poorer types of humanity, the sup-
pression of aesthetic creativeness. Without doubt these are
evils, dangerous and threatening. But they are not new.
From the dawn of history mankind has always been losing
its religious faith, has always suffered from the malignant
use of material power, has always suffered from the in-
fertility of its best intellectual types, has always witnessed
the periodical decadence of art . . . if we attend to what
actually has happened in the past, and disregard romantic
visions of democracies, aristocracies, kings, generals,
armies, and merchants, material power has generally been
wielded with blindness, obstinacy and selfishness, often
with brutal malignancy. And yet mankind has progressed.

Whitehead goes on almost immediately to tell us that 'The problem is not how to produce great men, but how to produce great societies. The great society will put up the men for the occasions.' This I find both puzzling and discouraging. I even doubt whether it is true. It seems to me our ethics are far advanced, and I do not know how often even great societies have failed to produce great men when they needed them. But principally the creation of great societies, unless it arises from the development of great men, seems out of our present range. Toynbee[6] says, after discussing various theories of man and society, 'Society is a "field of action", but the *source* of all action is the individuals composing it.' This suits me better.

There is also the hope that truth will prevail. If the relativistic as opposed to the positivistic philosophy is a true philosophy, it may be that in the course of time truth will meet with convincing acceptance. Its great triumph in the field of the natural sciences seems to indicate that it will. Bacon's idea of the 'binding of Proteus', that is, the idea that controlled experiment as a means of establishing truth must have seemed to the scientists of his day a mere idea or a mere commonplace, but it turned out to be a great true principle, and the results of its application are known to all the world. The doctrine of the rights of man, what we call the Bill of Rights, was advanced in the seventeenth century as a correct and effective principle of government. It grew in strength during the eighteenth century and was accepted during the nineteenth all over the English-speaking world, and in our century both in the Covenant of the League of Nations and the Charter of the United Nations it has been submitted to the judgement of the world. It looks as if it were a true principle in a just, lasting and harmonious government of man in society. How many true principles tending towards human happiness and the welfare of civilization in that and other fields have been propounded and rejected or neglected one does not know, but one thinks that there have probably been a great many. The beneficent principle of free trade has not been doing well in the public mind for two generations, although recent developments seem to indicate that it has not been everywhere rejected. Acceptance and rejection of truth probably form a continuum affected by various factors and possibly weighted in civilized countries in favour of acceptance.

Therefore there is a chance, in view of its highly auspicious, learned and independent origin, that the philosophy of relativism will, as time goes on, gradually meet with acceptance in other fields besides physical science. It has been said that in view of its naturalness and with the assistance of symbolic logic it may work great changes for the better in discursive fields. If so, we may conjecture that when all related subjects have accepted it, and, in spite of its initial difficulties of comprehension, scholars in literature, let us say Shakespeare scholars, will slowly and tentatively adopt it.

The idea insisted on in this book, that of scholarship broadly conceived, derived from an understanding that rests content with nothing short of the completest possible conception of the actual, demanding breadth of interests and characterized by what may be described as enlightened common sense, is the main hope for the acceptance of an appropriate relativism in place of an improperly extended positivism. It is admitted that it will at first be accepted and acted upon by great scholars only, and the reason for this is that they have always, often unconsciously, complied with it in their procedure. Their works show that they have. Scholarship is not one positive thing. It is a calling or occupation, and, like all professions, it has its art and its varying value. It is said to be good or bad. It may be devoted to compilation, to definition, or to interpretation. It seeks the truth with reference to obscure or doubtful issues, or it may seek discoveries or evidences of truth. It, like art itself, is subject not only to changes in style, method and purpose, but to conventionalization. I presume it is a continuum with a point of normal efficacy; one dictionary defines it as the systemized knowledge or activity of a learned man in quest of truth, exhibiting accuracy, critical ability and thoroughness. If scholarship follows a wrong method that results in partial truth or becomes a convention devoted to the establishment of authority or of erroneous theory, one would like to say that it is no longer scholarship, but this is not true; it is merely bad scholarship.

In this connection it is not necessary to make a catalogue of great scholars, but for the sake of clarity one might mention a few familiar names. It is generally agreed that Edmund Malone was a great scholar. He showed that Shakespeare was not an isolated genius but one of a group of great Elizabethan dramatists, he made a list of Shakespeare's plays in order of their composition that, with a few exceptions, still stands, he showed acumen in the detection of forgeries, illuminated the text of Shakespeare by his mastery of language, and was a critic of no mean ability. I omit many names. A man I saw and heard lecture a few times, C. H. Herford, impressed me as a great and well-rounded scholar, a thinker and a man of delicate perception—a critic of great erudition and excellent prose style. I heard lectures by A. S. Napier on *The*

History of the Holy Roodtree and on *Sir Gawain and the Green Knight,* and I still look back with wonder on Napier's mastery of Germanic philology. One of the greatest of scholars in the older tradition was certainly Sir Edmund Chambers. To convince the reader I need only point to his work on Elizabethan drama and ask if he does not fulfil the requirements of the dictionary? Did he not possess the 'systemized knowledge and activity of a learned man in quest of truth, exhibiting accuracy, critical ability and thoroughness'? I saw G. L. Kittredge only casually, but I knew the power and versatility of his mind and the greatness of his influence. May I also mention my own teacher, John Matthews Manly? I could go much further, but I have gone far enough to say that these men did not talk about books until they knew the books they talked about, knew them from every angle. There was the famous era of European liberal scholarship in the later seventeenth century, and I have an idea that there was another in the late nineteenth century while the *Dictionary of National Biography* was being compiled. The great collections of manuscripts in the British Museum and the Bodley have gathered dust since those days, days before the era of specialization, dogmatism and modernism. This is not to say that there have not been many great scholars in the humanistic field since the times referred to. The question is, did not and do not the greatest of later scholars follow the broad principles of all scholarship regarded historically as great? Have they not eschewed the dogmatism of the scientific method applied to literature? The answer is that they must if they are to find the truth.

There are reasons for this turn of affairs. The scientific method almost forced twentieth-century generations to become specialists. It was a fashionable thing to do and the best road to a doctor's degree. Specialization was also greatly promoted by the course of study: no classics, little foreign literature, little history, no philosophy, and largely things about literature instead of literature itself. No wonder so many humanistic scholars became specialists or sometimes exemplified the strange paradox of the man who, having rejected all learning, claimed to know everything. Let us not forget, however, that many of them escaped the error of over-specialization in discursive fields.

The question I have raised and wish to have candidly and objectively considered is this: are not the characteristics of great scholarship—breadth of view, accuracy of knowledge, sound judgement, and appreciation of meaning—exactly those demanded by the new philosophy of relativism? I merely express the opinion that literature, as a discursive subject, does not yield itself satisfactorily to experiment and the scientific method, but must perforce rely on experience, which is an approach essentially inductive. This philosophy restricts positivism to the limited area to which it belongs. It provides freedom from the conjectural or *a priori* approach and provides, at the same time, by means of symbolic logic, the possibility of safe generalization on high levels of abstraction. Does it not also detect and correct anachronism?

Take, for example, the obsession of critics and commentators with character. From the philosophy of the space-time continuum character must be as infinitely varied as human faces and physiognomies. One would not deny that certain modern writers have, by use of their knowledge of men and women, actually invented characters, so that character depiction became a conscious process of synthesis. But writers before Samuel Richardson did not produce their people that way.

They always worked from life, except of course for a limited number of inherited types. They rarely invented plots, for event was God's affair, as were characters. To waste volumes on Shakespeare's characters is anachronistic, if not absurd. Shakespeare prevailingly worked from event and presented character by inference from deeds and motives. The current idea seems to be that Shakespeare went to his cupboard full of pigeon-holes and took out his characters ready made. Thackeray may have done something of the sort with his 'Becky puppet', but not Shakespeare and the predecessors of Richardson and Fielding. Granted that in essential respects it often amounts to the same thing, ignorance is nevertheless a corruption as well as a deformity.

There is certainly some hope for the further decay of misleading tradition at least in enlightened circles. That the age-old misconception of both the Middle Ages and the Renaissance should be greatly changed is possibly too much to expect. A more natural and more realistic philosophy might do something, as time goes on, in that direction, but for a long time Hamlet will continue to be merely a synonym for procrastination, Shakespeare will be a poacher and the son of a butcher, and the Middle Ages will continue to be the Dark Ages.

I have known since college days that, as a result of Descartes' division of the total environment into matter and spirit (really the identification of matter with actuality) that, in the development of the method of science, discursive subjects suffered injury in being regarded as areas about which nothing in the way of truth could be known. It is therefore a gratification to find a clear statement of the facts by a distinguished modern writer on philosophy and logic. Susanne

Langer in *Philosophy in a New Key*[7] speaks in this way:

> As the physical world-picture grew and technology advanced, those disciplines which rested squarely on 'rational' instead of 'empirical' principles were threatened with complete extinction, and were soon denied the honourable name of science. Logic and metaphysics, aesthetics and ethics, seemed to have seen their day. One by one the various branches of philosophy—natural, mental, social or religious—set up as autonomous sciences; the natural ones with more hope and fanfare than actual achievement. The physical sciences found their stride without much hesitation; psychology and sociology tried hard and seriously to 'catch the tune and keep the step', but with mathematical laws they were never really handy. . . .
>
> Yes, the heyday of science has stifled and killed our rather worn-out philosophical interests, born three and a half centuries ago from that great generative idea, the bifurcation of nature into an inner and an outer world. To the generations of Comte, Mill, and Spencer, it certainly seemed as though all human knowledge could be cast in the new mould; certainly as though nothing in any other mould could hope to jell. And indeed, nothing much *has* jelled in any other mould; but neither have the non-physical disciplines been able to adopt and thrive on the scientific methods that did such wonders for physics and its obvious derivations. The truth is that science has not really fructified and activated *all* human thought. . . .

The author then proceeds to attack with clarity and skill the problem of knowledge from the point of view of symbolization and other philosophic approaches.

In this book it has been suggested that the scientific method, although sound and productive in tangible areas, is inadequate except to some degree in factual areas for the exploitation of discursive subjects. It has also been suggested that the new epistemology itself is suited to the discovery of truth and that, with the aid of symbolic logic, it may in time bring about advance-

ment in these fields. It has also been suggested that it
was a mistake for such subjects to hand themselves
over without recourse to the positivistic method of
science.

This can perhaps be made more clear. Civilization
has not been without truth or utterly dependent on
revelation for it. What we have known about human
welfare (what is called wisdom) and followed to our
profit is not made up of unsupported speculations. We
have been dependent on the Hebrew prophets and the
Greek philosophers, who had no scientific method.
They applied their natural powers of perception and
cognition to their knowledge and experience. Possibly
wisdom and virtue belong to an evolutionary series,
I don't know, but we seem to have got along fairly
well before we began to prefer science to wisdom. In
any case, there can surely be no doubt that the greater
concepts on which our civilization has been based
were true. This is a very general statement, which
should be expanded to include the idea that such
things as manners, morals, religion, economic and
political principles, and literature need not remain
either unintelligible or subject to heterogeneous or
inappropriate empiricism. It has been suggested that
there is now a philosophy that seems by its freedom
and naturalness to open these fields to orderly consideration. That the investigation may be slow as well
as tardy there is no doubt, and the question arises, is
the learned body of our society able and willing to
make a great attempt?

Literature and language, particularly English language and literature, present an interesting case. Possibly because it was thought that language was unimportant and literature might serve only for the re-
laxation and entertainment for the idle hours of men

who had something really important to do in the world, English was late in being admitted to the *studium generale*. Language as a science led off, and in phonology and morphology did well, and, if its investigation had been broader and more persistent, its progress might have continued and reached more quickly, and even surpassed, its present philosophical conceptions.

In literature, mainly in this century, a distressing thing has happened. It may be due to its adoption of the positivistic philosophy of science. Criticism and even the literary interpretation of scholars has widely adopted and applied a dogmatic or *a priori* point of view that has resulted in the avoidance of experience, that is, the avoidance of literature itself. The only hope again lies in the work of great scholars. There is encouragement, for example in the high degree of development to be seen in the scholarship of Chaucer and Spenser and of some other authors and periods. The vast field of Shakespeare, with its irresistible appeal and importance, has had the attention of many great scholars, but is still strangely disordered by conjecture, avoidance and dogmatism.

The new epistemology in its breadth and naturalness seems to promise freedom from hampering intellectual restrictions and in general. Some faith, I hope not altogether mystical, was expressed above in freedom as an eternal idea and a generating agent. Our hope for great advancement in the study of our subject, nothing less than a renascence in fact, might find in freedom a motivating force for such a development. We find ourselves confronted by a world diverted from true learning by commercialism and the indifference that it engenders, a world non-participant in both the search for truth and in literary creativity; we find ourselves relying on such old-fashioned things as the ultimate prevalence of truth, belief in what ordinary people will do if set free from intellectual restrictions, and in industry and common sense.

When we think of the difficulties in the way of a renascence of arts and letters in the modern world, we are tempted to throw up our hands in despair. Ignorance and indifference confront us and we see the blind leading the blind. Ignorance and error seem well organized and supported. There are assertive groups of complacent and self-adulatory scholars who defend our inadequate and static position and defend it dangerously. 'We,' they say, 'are a renascence.' In a certain pragmatical sense they may be right and we wrong. There are also large and potent groups whose ontology is erroneous, if not superstitious. There are moreover real perplexities, great and small. For example, there is the problem of Parmenos and his pig. Parmeno was a Roman actor whose competitor could squeal like a pig. Parmenos brought under his cloak a real pig on the boards and tormented it so that it squealed in rivalry with his competitor; but, when he did so, the audience hissed Parmenos from the stage, pig and all. I see the point, but my sympathies have always been with the pig, since squealing is the business of pigs, and I have no doubt that they squeal with greater or less effectiveness. I even entertain the possibly perverted idea that the point in the continuum where art and nature come closest together is the norm. I am on the side of nature against artifice and on the side of literature against commentary on literature.

Nevertheless, there remains the belief that the philosophy of a people or a group is the most important thing about them. There is precedent for believing that a better philosophy both inspires and rectifies. Therefore this book has suggested that students of the humanities would do well to amplify and correct their scientific beliefs and procedures by means of the broader and more naturalistic philosophy of relativism and thus confine positivism within its reasonable limits. In spite of this enumeration of hopes and hindrances I still believe that there is before the learned world at this time a new direction and that there is a bare chance that we may have in our subject, as in others, a re-birth. We must abandon the sole, stringent use of the scientific method, particularly the errors into which it entices us—truncated inductions, invented causes and the positivistic attitudes. But the pedagogical experience of a lifetime makes me add that error is not corrected by debate. We must broaden our minds, master what the modern learned world has to offer, and thus arrive at an epistemology suited to the acquisition of truth in our at least largely discursive field. Such a conception will of itself mitigate or destroy the errors. Ideas, as we know, sometimes have great potency, and it is possible that there is a new and true one abroad in the world. It might take hold and spread. Meantime, let us remember that we are not Atlases and that we do not have to hold up the entire earth. And so we end with Milton: 'Let her and Falsehood grapple; who ever knew Truth put to the worse, in a free and open encounter?'

The greatest needs of the modern world cannot be supplied from super-markets. We need honest, industrious and patriotic men, intelligent and faithful wives and mothers, and children who are not delinquent. This is another way of saying that we need to know more about how these blessings can be achieved. It may be only a dream, but if we had freedom, a sounder philosophy leading to the mastery of these difficult ideals and greater knowledge, faith and wisdom, we might make inroads on these difficult but essential territories and by the power of God's truth bring about in discursive fields a renascence comparable to that of science and technology.

BIBLIOGRAPHICAL NOTES

CHAPTER I

[1] I have not been able to find any authoritative treatment of the relativistic theory of cognition. Some information will be found in Einstein's *The Meaning of Relativity* (Princeton, 1950) and *Out of my Later Years* (New York, 1950); also in *The Evolution of Physics* by Einstein and Infeld (New York, 1942). There are references in the various works of Whitehead, and of course Herman Minkowsky's *Erde und Zeit* (1907) is fundamental. See also *Contemporary Approaches to Cognition*. Colorado Symposium (Cambridge, Mass., 1957).

[2] Woodrow Wilson entertained an almost mystical belief in the individual and social efficacy of liberty, or at least one may say that to him freedom was an eternal idea of supreme importance. This appears in reports of Wilson's 1912 campaign for election to the presidency of the United States. These are to be found in *The New Freedom; a Call for the Emancipation of the Generous Energies of a People,* compiled by W. B. Hale from the author's campaign speeches (New York, 1913), and in a better version in *A Crossroads of Freedom; the 1912 campaign speeches of Woodrow Wilson,* ed. J. W. Davidson (New Haven, 1956).

[3] Susanne Langer, *Philosophy in a New Key* (New York, 1948), with bibliography; C. K. Ogden and I. A. Richards, *The Meaning of Meaning* (London, 1923); *Die Philosophie der symbolischen Formen.* 3 vols. (Berlin, 1923, 1924, 1929); Rudolf Carnap, *Meaning and Change of Meaning* (London, 1935); A. N. Whitehead, *Symbolism, its Meaning and Effect* (New York, 1927).

[4] C. D. Broad, *The Philosophy of Francis Bacon* (Cambridge, 1926).

[5] One of the best ways of arriving at an understanding of Baconian induction, its nature and claims as an epistemological method, is to consult the works of actual proponents

of the system rather than the more critical recent historians
of philosophy. I suggest the writings of James McCosh,
which are clear and far advanced, such as *The Institutions
of the Mind Inductively Investigated* (1860), *An Examination
of Mr. J. S. Mill's Philosophy* (1866), *The Laws of Discursive Thought* (1870), and *Christianity and Positivism* (1871).

[6] A good deal of Lowes' important work on Chaucer is in
the form of articles in learned journals. He published,
however, *The Art of Geoffrey Chaucer* in 1931 and *Geoffrey
Chaucer and the Development of his Genius* in 1934. An
earlier work, *Convention and Revolt in Poetry* (1919) bears
some relation to *The Road to Xanadu*.

[7] The text of *The Road to Xanadu*, published by The
Vintage Press, New York, 1959.

[8] *Loc. cit.*, p. 95.

[9] *Ibid.*, pp. 57-8, 396.

[10] *Ibid.*, pp. 52, 55, 63; Henry James, *Works*, II, p. vi, New
York Edition.

[11] *Loc. cit.*, p. 60.

[12] *Complete Works*, ed. James A. Harrison (1902), Vol. XIV,
p. 73.

[13] *The Road to Xanadu, loc. cit.*, pp. 67, 100.

[14] *Ibid.*, pp. 220, 325, 104.

[15] *Ibid.*, p. 350.

[16] *Science and the Modern World* (New York, 1925; Cambridge, 1926); see also *The Philosophy of Alfred North
Whitehead*, ed. by Paul A. Schilpp (Evanston, 1941).

[17] Samuel Alexander, *Space, Time, and Deity* (London, 1920;
New York, 1950).

[18] *Modern Science and the Modern Man* (New York, 1952),
pp. 69-71.

[19] Second edition revised, New York, 1953.

[20] Pp. 174, 176, 178, 179-80.

[21] Pp. 180, 182, 184, 190, 191-2.

[22] Pp. 194, 196.

CHAPTER II

[1] See Whitehead, *Process and Reality*, pp. 38, 129-30, 251-2,
335-6 *et passim*. The following statement, sub-head xxv
under the Categories of Explanation, states Whitehead's

doctrine: 'The final phase in the process of concrescence, constituting an actual entity, is one complex, fully determinate feeling. This final phase is termed the "satisfaction". It is fully determinate (*a*) as to its genesis, (*b*) as to its objective character for the transcendent creativity, and (*c*) as to its prehension—positive or negative—of every item in its universe.'

2 *Harvard Studies in Classical Philology*, Vol. XXVII (1916), pp. 1-65.

3 P. 45.

4 This perennial conflict—in the age of Jonson and Dryden and by revival in the time of Matthew Arnold—is, in our view, insignificant except in so far as it has substituted debate for thought and operated restrictively.

5 S. H. Butcher, *Aristotle's Theory of Poetry and Fine Art, with a Critical Text and a Translation of the Poetics* (London, 1885); Lane Cooper, *Aristotle on the Art of Poetry* (New York, 1913; Ithaca, 1947).

6 *Op. cit.*, pp. 31, 33.

7 New York, 1943, 1959.

8 Edition of 1959, p. 129.

9 *Epistolae Obscurorum Virorum*. The Latin text with an English rendering, notes and an historical introduction by Francis Griffin Stokes (London, 1909). Attention is called to the introduction.

10 *Die Hartzreise* (earlier pages). *Sämtliche Werke*, Bd. 4 (Leipzig, 1912).

11 *History of Ethics within Organized Christianity* (New York, 1910), pp. 433-7.

CHAPTER III

1 See *Adventures of Ideas* (New York, 1955), pp. 23-5, 150-1, *et passim*; also *Science and the Modern World, loc. cit.*, pp. 88 ff., *et passim*.

2 Boston, 1923.

3 *Canterbury Tales*, Group E. VI, ll. 30-4.

4 *Othello*, V, ii, 11.

5 *The Faerie Queene*, book II, canto ix, stanzas 44-60.

6 London, 1925.

7 Ithaca, 1944.

8 *Science and the Modern World, loc. cit.*, p. 152.

CHAPTER IV

[1] Such works in superior form are the Cambridge and Oxford histories of English literature.

[2] Friedrich Klaeber, *The Later Genesis and Other Old English and Old Saxon Texts relating to the Fall of Man* (Heidelberg, 1913, 1931); with bibliography.

[3] *The Enchanted Glass* (New York, 1936; Oxford, 1950), pp. 95-6.

[4] On this basis Bacon built *The Wisdom of the Ancients* (1619).

[5] Karl Young, *The Drama of the Mediaeval Church* (2 v. Oxford, 1933), II, 276-303.

[6] *Ibid.*, II, 369-86.

[7] Misplaced positivism seems to be an illustration of what Whitehead calls the Fallacy of Misplaced Concreteness. See *Science and the Modern World, loc. cit.*, pp. 52-9.

[8] For the works of Chaucer referred to in this paragraph see *The Complete Works of Geoffrey Chaucer,* ed. F. N. Robinson (Boston, 1933), III, (D), 832-1264, IV (E), 57-1244; V (F), 729-1624; also p. 631.

[9] See *A Literary History of England,* ed. A. C. Baugh (New York, 1948) with bibliography. The three versions of *Piers the Plowman* were edited by W. W. Skeat for E.E.T.S., 1867-84.

[10] See 'An Unpublished Introduction to *Babbitt*' in *The Man from Main Street* (New York, 1953).

[11] See *Chief Pre-Shakespearean Dramas,* ed. Joseph Quincy Adams (Boston, 1924), pp. 638-65.

[12] *An Essay on Criticism,* ll. 201-14.

[13] *The Spectator,* No. 1, dated March 1, 1710/11.

[14] *Characteristics: An Inquiry concerning Virtue or Merit,* bk. I, pt. iii, sect. 1.

CHAPTER V

[1] William James, *The Principles of Psychology* (2 v. New York, 1890), pp. 224-90.

[2] Whitehead, *Science and the Modern World, loc. cit.*, pp. 175-8; *Process and Reality, loc. cit.*, 442-3, *et passim*.

[3] Sir E. K. Chambers, *The Mediaeval Stage* (2 v. Oxford, 1903), II, 1-67; Karl Young, *op. cit.*, I, 178-410, *et passim*.

[4] 'Literary Forms and the New Theory of the Origin of Species,' *Modern Philology*, IV (1906-7), 577-95.

[5] Gardner Murray, *An Historical Introduction to Modern Psychology* (London, 1928, 1948), pp. 29-30, 55-9, 226-34, 408.

[6] See chapter II above.

[7] See particularly *Prefaces to Shakespeare* (2 v. Princeton, 1946), I, 1-23, and discussion of the nature and constitution of various plays and of the issues confronting various characters.

[8] *Poetics*, VI, 9-10: For Tragedy is an imitation, not of men, but of an action and of life and life consists in action, and its end is a mode of action, not a quality. Now character determines men's qualities, but it is by their actions that they are happy or the reverse. Dramatic action, therefore, is not with a view to the representation of character: character comes in as a subsidiary to the actions. Hence the incidents and the plot are the end of a tragedy; and the end itself is the chief thing of all. (Butcher's translation.)

[9] The famous passage itself (*Poetics*, VI, 23), often the only part known to writers on drama, provides, if read carefully, agreement between the doctrines of Aristotle and the practice of Shakespeare: Tragedy, then, is an imitation of an action that is serious, complete, and of a certain magnitude; in language embellished with each kind of artistic ornament, the several kinds being found in separate parts of the play; in the form of action, not of narrative; through pity and fear affecting the purgation of these emotions. (Butcher's translation.)

[10] *Wilhelm Meister*, bk. v.

[11] *Notes and Lectures upon Shakespeare* (New York, 1868), IV, 144.

[12] Act II, sc. ii, ll. 129-59.

[13] Act I, sc. v, ll. 92-105.

[14] Act II, sc. ii, ll. 617-34.

[15] Act III, sc. i, ll. 56-88.

[16] Act III, sc. iv, ll. 73-96.

[17] Act III, sc. iv, ll. 31-2.

[18] Act IV, sc. iv, ll. 32-66.

[19] Act V, sc. iv, ll. 71-4.

[20] Act V, sc. ii, ll. 218-36.

CHAPTER VI

[1] Jacob Burckhardt, *The Civilization of the Renaissance in Italy*. Tr. S. C. G. Middlemore. (Vienna, 1937), pp. 146-85, *et passim*.

[2] Roger Ascham, *The Whole Works of Roger Ascham* (3 v. London, 1864), *The Scholemaster*, Vol. III, pp. 133-4.

[3] M. M. Knappen, *Tudor Puritanism* (Chicago, 1939), bk. I, sects ii-iv, *et passim*.

[4] T. W. Baldwin, *William Shakspere's Small Latine and Lesse Greeke* (2 v. Urbana, 1944).

[5] Of the many works on historiography I suggest Gilbert J. Garraghan, *A Guide to Historical Method* (New York, 1956) and Marc Bloch, *The Historian's Craft* (New York, 1953). J. H. Wigmore on the law of evidence will be found significant.

[6] Susanne Langer, *An Introduction to Symbolic Logic* (New York, 1953); C. I. Lewis and C. H. Langford, *Symbolic Logic* (New York, 1932); A. N. Whitehead and Lord Russell, *Principia Mathematica* (Cambridge, 1925), sections A and B; also A. De Morgan, *Formal Logic* (London, 1847) and G. Boole, *An Investigation of the Laws of Thought* (Chicago, 1916).

[7] J. W. Mackail, *The Approach to Shakespeare* (Oxford, 1930) and various histories of Elizabethan drama.

[8] R. B. McKerrow, *An Introduction to Bibliography for Literary Students* (Oxford, 1927); Sir Edmund Chambers, *William Shakespeare: A Study of Facts and Problems* (2 v. Oxford, 1930); Sir Walter Greg, *The Editorial Problem in in Shakespeare* (Oxford, 1951); *A Companion to Shakespeare Studies*, ed. Harley Granville-Barker and G. B. Harrison (Cambridge, 1934); also *Aspects of Shakespeare*, a collection of Shakespeare lectures before the British Academy, several of which have bearings on methods of textual study; see also J. D. Wilson's 'Textual Introduction to *The Tempest*, (Cambridge, 1921), and F. P. Wilson, 'Shakespeare and the New Bibliography,' in *Studies in Retrospect*, 1892-1942. Bibliographical Society (1945), pp. 76-135.

CHAPTER VII

[1] *Loc. cit.*, pp. 78 ff.

[2] *Complete Poetical Works of William Wordsworth* (London,

1909), Appendix, pp. 851-61; see also Wordsworth's *Literary Criticism*, ed. N. C. Smith (London, 1925), *passim*; Coleridge, *Biographia Literaria*, chs. IV, XIV, XVII, XX, XXII.

³ *Ibid.*, p. 152; see also *Coleridge's Literary Criticism*, ed. J. W. Mackail (1908 e.s. 1949).

⁴ A. W. Pollard, *Shakespeare's Folios and Quartos* (London, 1909) and 'The Foundations of Shakespeare's Text', *Proceedings of the British Academy*, XI (1923); R. B. McKerrow, *Introduction to Bibliography for Literary Students*, loc. cit.; *Prolegomena for the Oxford Shakespeare* (Oxford, 1939); Sir Walter Greg, *The Editorial Problem in Shakespeare*, loc. cit., extensive bibliography.

⁵ Sir Walter Greg, *The Shakespeare First Folio* (Oxford, 1955); Alice Walker, *Textual Problems of the First Folio* (Cambridge, 1953); Leo Kirschbaum, *Shakespeare and the Stationers* (Columbus, 1953).

⁶ The general avoidance of Shakespear's actual human appeal in criticism and instruction is indeed a serious matter. As Lord Russell says, 'There is not the slightest use, either for young or old, in being well-informed *about* literature, knowing the dates of the poets, the names of their works, and so on. Everything that can be put into a handbook is worthless.' (*On Education Especially in Early Childhood*, 1926.)

⁷ Spoken by Messer Morello in the fourth book of *The Courtier*.

⁸ *Falloden Papers* (Boston, 1926), 'The Pleasures of Reading.' The earlier part of that essay describes in a simple and sensible way how modern living hinders reading.

⁹ A. N. Whitehead, *Adventures of Ideas*, loc. cit., pp. 53-4.

CHAPTER VIII

¹ A. N. Whitehead, *Science and the Modern World*, loc. cit., pp. 159-65; *Adventures of Ideas*, loc. cit., pp. 181-90 ff., *et passim*.

² *Adventures of Ideas*, loc. cit., pp. 185-90.

³ Thomas Sprat, *History of the Royal Society* (London, 1667); also histories of the Royal Society by Thomas Birch (1756-7), C. R. Weld (1848).

⁴ H. B. Wheatly (1905). See remarks on Dryden as a critic in Chapter VII above.

[5] See Chapter VII above. The critical literature on Words-worth, Coleridge, Shelley and the criticism of the Romantic period is very voluminous. The reader is referred to *Cambridge Bibliography of English Literature* (4 v. Cambridge, 1941) and Supplement (Cambridge, 1957).

[6] The doctrine of forms from Plato and Aristotle to the present time has occupied the minds of practically all literary critics. Attention is called to Chapter II above. The bibliographical task is hopeless, and again reference is made to the *Cambridge Bibliography of English Literature*. S. H. Butcher's *Aristotle's Theory of Poetry and Fine Art* (1895) is a work of fundamental importance. For a discriminating treatment of the mainly Italian Aristotelians see Madeleine Doran, *Endeavors of Art* (Madison, 1954). See also Vernon Hall, Jr., *Renaissance Literary Criticism* (New York, 1945) on the aristocratic bent of criticism in the age.

[7] Besides publication in collected works there are several special editions; see particularly those of A. S. Cook (1890) and J. C. Collins (1907). For Sidney himself see life by M. W. Wallace; also K. G. Myrick, *Sir Philip Sidney as a Literary Craftsman* (Cambridge, Mass., 1955).

[8] See Louis I. Bredvold, *The Intellectual Milieu of John Dryden* (Ann Arbor, 1934); H. J. C. Grierson, *Cross Currents in English Literature* (London, 1929); Hugh Macdonald, *John Dryden: a Bibliography* (Oxford, 1939).

[9] See the brief discussion of Wordsworth in the preceding chapter and the references cited there.

[10] Wir sehen eine Menge Menschen, ja ganze Nationen, so sehr befangen in den Gewöhnungen ihrer Erziehung und Lebenweise, dass sie sich auch dann nicht davon losreissen können, wenn vom Genusse schöner Kunst die Rede ist. Nur dasjenige, was in ihrer Sprache, ihren Sitten und ihren gesellschaftlichen Verhältnissen einheimisch und hergebracht ist, erscheint ihnen als natürlich, schicklich und schön. In dieser ausschliessenden Ansicht und Empfindungsweise kann man es durch Bildung zu einer grossen Feinheit der Unterscheidung in dem engen Kreise bringen, worauf man sich nun einmal beshränkt hat. Aber ein ächter Kenner kann man nicht sein ohne Universalität des Geistes, d.h. ohne die Biegsamkeit, welche uns in den Stand setzt, mit Verläugnung persönlicher Vorliebe und blinder Gewöhnung, uns in die Eigenheiten anderer Völker und Zeitalter zu versetzen, sie

glichsam aus ihren Mittelpunkte heraus zu fühlen, und
was die menschliche Natur adelt, alles Schöne und Grosse
unter den äusserlichen Zuthaten, deren es zu feiner Ver-
körperung bedarf, ja bisweilen unter befremdlich schei-
nenden Verkleidungen zu erkennen und gehörig zu wür-
digen. Es giebt kein Monopol der Poesie für gewisse
Zeitalter und Völker; folglich ist auch der Despotismus des
Geschmachts, womit diese gewisse vielleicht ganz willkürlich
bei ihnen festgestellte Regeln allgemein durchsetzen wollen,
immer eine ungültige Anmassung. Poesie, im weitesten
Sinne genommen, als die Fähigkeit das Schöne zu ersinnen
und es sichtbar oder hörbar darzustellen, ist eine allgemeine
Gabe des Himmels, und selbst sogenannte Barbaren und
Wilde haben nach ihrem Masse Antheil daran. (*Sammtliche
Werke,* hrsg. v. E. Böcking. Bd. 5, S. 4-5.)

[11] It is interesting to reflect before perhaps forty thousand
volumes of best-sellers stacked away on library shelves, as
I once did in the public library of the city of St. Paul,
Minnesota. The formal rules of critics, the ignorance of the
reading public and the vagaries of fashion must have passed
over without notice great numbers of fine works. It is not
possible to think so badly of humanity as to believe that
there is nothing worth noting on those shelves.

[12] One wonders what label critics, if they had ever heard of
him, would have attached to Wilhelm Dilthey.

CHAPTER IX

[1] This chapter makes use of an article in *Philological
Quarterly,* VII, 321-33 and of *The Enchanted Glass.*

[2] *Short History of the Renaissance in Italy* (New York, 1893),
pp. 7-18.

[3] *The Renaissance in Italy, loc. cit.,* Vol. II, pp. 4-10.

[4] Article on the Renaissance, *Encyclopaedia Britannica,* 11th
Edn., Vol. XXIII, pp. 83 ff.

[5] Vol. I, pp. 523-84.

[6] See *Cambridge History of English Literature,* Vol. IV, ch. 1,
'Translators' by Charles Whibley; also Vol. III, ch. 1,
'Englishmen and the Classical Renaissance' by T. M.
Lindsay; C. H. Conley, *The First English Translators of
the Classics* (New Haven, 1927); also Jebb, *loc. cit.,* pp.

579-80, where the author quotes Ascham's letter on the revival of learning at Cambridge; and J. A. Gee, *The Life and Works of Thomas Lupset* (New Haven, 1928), with references for a discussion of Fisher's and Fox's establishment of humanistic studies at Cambridge and Oxford respectively.

[7] *The Renaissance* (New York and London, n.d.), p. 8.

[8] Jacob Burckhardt, *The Civilization of the Renaissance in Italy, loc. cit.*, pp. 171-5, 359 ff.

[9] See, for example, J. J. Jusserand, *A Literary History of the English People* (London and New York, 1906), Vol. II, pp. 26-40.

[10] That the curriculum of the schools was as stated appears from the statutes of the University of Paris and by implication at least in many other documents. See Hastings Rashdell, *The Universities of Europe in the Middle Ages* (Oxford, 1895), Vol. I, pp. 433-62, *et passim*. An idea of what was actually done in preparation for examinations, the corpus of instruction, appears in *Margarita Philosophica* (Friburg, 1503; Strassburg, 1504 (bis), 1508, 1512, 1515; Basle, 1508, 1517, 1523?, 1535, 1583; Venice, 1599, Italian translation). This vastly popular work presents complete treatises on grammar, logic, rhetoric, arithmethic, music, geometry, and astronomy (to which is added astrology), together with Philosophia triceps: Naturalis, Rationalis and Moralis. Vives protests against the use of such secondary works as these *Margaritae*. See Foster Watson, *Vives: On Education* (Cambridge, 1913), p. cviii.

[11] The *Heptaplus* of Pico della Mirandola presents such an organization. A threefold division of essences, angelic or intelligible, celestial and sublunary, with man the microcosm constitute the universe. He gives throughout a metaphysical interpretation of the Ptolemaic cosmogony, with correspondences, and adds the Christian concept of a heaven with the Pseudo-Dionysiac nine orders of angels with their correspondences. He applies his gigantic scheme to the Mosaic genesis.

[12] Ramus was translated into English three times before 1640: M. R. Makylmenaeum, 1574; A. Wotton, 1626; R. Fage, 1632.

[13] The *Dictes* was issued four times by Caxton: 1477 bis, 1480?, 1489, and once by Wynkyn de Worde, 1528, and the same interest was carried on by William Baldwin and Thomas

Palfreyman, jointly and severally, in the middle of the sixteenth century and extending well into the seventeenth
century and amounted to about thirty publications. We must
add to this strange basis for renascence the Distiches of Cato
and the *Chiliades* of Erasmus.

[14] *The Ethiques of Aristotle,* trans. J. Wilkinson, 1547.

[15] The basis of this political trend is a catalogue of books in-
cluding these: Laurence Humphrey, *The Nobles, or Of
Nobilitye,* 1563; Matthieu Coignet, *Politique Discourse upon
Trueth and Lying,* trans. Hoby, 1586; La Primaudaye, *The
French Adademie,* trans. Bowes, 1586, 1589, 1594, 1602, 1614,
1618; Philippe de Mornay, *The True Knowledge of a Mans
owne selfe,* trans. A. Munday, 1602; R. Nannini, *Civil
Considerations,* trans. from the French of Chappuys by
W. T., 1601; Girolamo Cardano, *Cardanus Comforte,* trans.
Bedingfield, 1573, 1576; Lodowick Bryskett, *A Discourse of
Civill Life,* 1606; T. Blundeville, *Three Morall Treatises*
(from the *Moralia* of Plutarch), 1580; G. du Vair, *The Moral
Philosophie of the Stoicks,* trans. T. James (?), 1597; Sir
Richard Barckley, *A Discourse of the Felicitie of Man,* 1603,
1631.

[16] See Lewis Einstein, *The Italian Renaissance in England*
(New York, 1913), pp. 245 ff.

[17] Chapman's frank embodiment in his plays of European
political as well as ethical theory has been studied by
Franck L. Schoell, *Études sur l'humanisme continental en
Angleterre à la fin de la Renaissance* (Paris, 1926).

[18] In *Batman uppon Bartholome* (1582) only minor and unimportant changes are found.

[19] See *Robert Burton and The Anatomy of Melancholy,* ed.
F. Madan, which is made up of papers by various scholars
(Oxford, 1926).

CHAPTER X

[1] *The Grammar of Science* (London, 1900), pp. 96-100, *et
passim.*

[2] There is of course *The Idea of Progress* by J. B. Bury
(London, 1920) and a large number of books and articles
on the subject. An idea of trends of opinion can be gathered
from *A Century of Progress,* a volume of collected essays
edited by C. A. Beard (New York, 1953).

[3] There are of course other expressions in Sir Winston Churchill's post-war speeches of belief in the ultimate victory of human freedom.

[4] *A Study of History* (New York, 1949), p. 554.

[5] *Science and the Modern World, loc. cit.,* p. 204.

[6] *Op. cit.,* p. 211.

[7] *Philosophy in a New Key, loc. cit.,* pp. 12-13.

INDEX